Flip-Flops
After 50

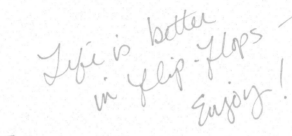

Life is better
in flip-flops —
Enjoy!

Flip-Flops
After 50

*And Other Thoughts on Aging
I Remembered to Write Down*

Cindy Eastman

Cindy Eastman

SwP
SHE WRITES PRESS

Published 2014
Printed in the United States of America
ISBN: 978-1-938314-68-1
Library of Congress Control Number: 2013951190

For information, address:
She Writes Press
1563 Solano Ave #546
Berkeley, CA 94707

For the island

Contents

All Grown Up

Introduction

The Year of Thinking BIG. That is my theme for the next couple of years. So I guess, more accurately, my theme should be The Years of Thinking BIG, but let's not quibble over an "s." As I approach a certain age (no big mystery: fifty), I am developing a philosophy that is not dependent on what people think of me anymore. I am much more concerned these days with what I think of me and how I'll be thinking of me in the years to come. And as I reach this place in my life where people normally start thinking about retirement and counting up the various nest eggs they've laid over the years, all I can think about is how I've laid only one big fat egg in that department. Because of various traumatic and irresponsible events in my life, I don't have a retirement plan. To be honest, I don't even have any kind of plan, except that one day I'd like to be in the retirement phase of my life.

I look at retirement as a time to travel, garden, read, and basically enjoy life. I know it sounds like an AARP slogan, but it becomes meaningful after one enters her late forties. After years of working under conditions set forth by others, it has suddenly become far more important to me to be able to live under conditions set forth by me. This means being able to sleep in when I'm tired, go up to Maine when I feel like it, not drive in the cold and the snow to get somewhere someone else thinks I should be. It also means making flip-flops my main footwear. If I can't wear flip-flops to a place, it's probably not a place I want to go. I have "good" flip-flops (those I clean up after each wearing) and "everyday" flip-flops (which I don't). These allow me to enjoy a wide spectrum of events. So, that's my goal: flip-flops after fifty. I think it's doable.

Of course, this means that I now need a retirement plan. Since I want to work from home and don't want to run a daycare or start a business on eBay, and since the one thing I can do well is write, I need to make a commitment to my writing: it must become a discipline, and I must make it an important part of my daily routine. This becomes difficult when one holds a nine-to-five, five-day-a-week job. Or, as it's been lately, a seven-to-six, six-day-a-week job. But this is The Year of Thinking BIG! I must press on. So there's that: stick to my writing. I don't know how I will make it pay for my retirement, but who knows what will come down the pike?

I'm brewing another couple of ideas, too. All are connected to writing, and some have to do with education. After all, I didn't go back to school and rack up tens of thousands of dollars in debt earning a master's degree for nothing. All in all, I think I might be onto something. Planning for retirement: what a concept.

For a long time I've trudged along the path of Do the Right Thing. I've held jobs and paid taxes and registered and insured my cars. I sent my kids to school with lunch every day, helped them with their homework, and took out loans to pay for their higher education. If I didn't have anything nice to say, I didn't say it. If I took a penny, I left a penny. I'm not saying my new philosophy will change all this, but I do think that after almost fifty years of following the rules, I can safely assume I can be trusted to behave. The way I see it, I am able, motivated, smart, and ready. What's to stop me?

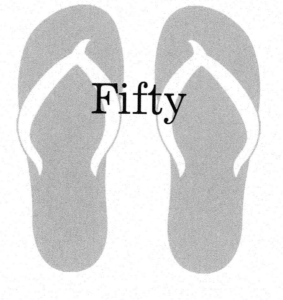

Fifty

The Year of Living Fifty-ishly

In 2008, I joined such illustrious company as Holly Hunter, Alec Baldwin, Michelle Pfeiffer, LEGO, AARP, Alpha-Bits, the Rolodex, and Jif peanut butter. How? We all turned fifty.

Turning fifty is no big deal if you're, say, the Interstate Highway System, which turned fifty in 2006. In fact, you *should* be fifty if you're the Interstate Highway System—it gives you a certain air of respectability and responsibility. But when you're a woman who still feels like she's, oh, in her late thirties, it can be a little more frightening. Not scary frightening (as in not one but *two* terms of George Bush), just slightly frightening (as in where the hell is the how-to guide for turning fifty?).

For me, approaching fifty was just plain mind-boggling. In the preceding months, as I wrote journal entries and notes to myself regarding my upcoming birthday ("For my fiftieth birthday . . . " or "Can I find a new job at fifty?"), I would stop and look at what I'd written, and I felt as if I were lying about my age, but in the reverse. How could I possibly be this old?

AARP knew I was turning fifty practically before I did. They started the campaign to get me into their little cult about six months earlier, sending me an application for membership and a subscription to their magazine. I guess they wanted to be sure I remembered to join. So I did. Why not? Who doesn't want to be a member of an organization whose cover girl is Caroline Kennedy or whose cover boy is Kevin Costner? I'm game—count me in.

It's not that I wasn't ready to be fifty. I don't mind aging. I don't look or feel old. One of my vain little secrets is that I absolutely love it when I tell people how old my oldest child is and they say, "*What? You don't look like you have a child that old!*" or when the guy at Starbucks says, "She's your mom? I thought you were sisters!" when I stop in for coffee with my daughter, Annie. (I'm sure Annie loves that one as much as I do.)

For the most part, I was okay with the whole thing. But there are intrinsic elements to turning fifty that have to be addressed. It is certainly a time for reflection and stocktaking. Reflection is okay: I feel lucky that I am in good health, that I'm living my life in a way I can be proud of, and that I have raised amazing children. I am married to a good man who also raised a wonderful daughter and who lives his life in a mindful and generous way. My parents are healthy, and so are my brother and sister, and we all enjoy a fairly sane and loving familial relationship. My friends are few, but they're steadfast and fun, and I can call any one of them in a pinch. (Like if I'm freaking out about turning fifty. Which I'm not.) And there's the above-mentioned looking good for my age—which doesn't hurt. Sure, I could stand to lose a few pounds, but who couldn't?

It's the other thing, the stock-taking part, that I'm having the teeniest bit of trouble with. The part where I look back on my life and check to see if I've gotten most of the things done that I've always wanted to do. The answer is no. And when you're fifty and the answer is no, a new time frame is suddenly in place. I have only so many years left to travel to Greece, Italy, and Australia or to drive an RV across the United States. I have only so much time to live in New York City or start my own business. But the biggest thing—the thing I imposed my own time limit on—was becoming a Writer and Getting Published. I set a deadline of age fifty to get published, and I didn't meet my goal. But don't fret. I'm not leaving things at a potentially depressing point. If life is all about the journey rather than the destination, then at this point I'm just getting more information about the remaining trip. Turning fifty is like stopping at a travel center to check the map and maybe get a cup of coffee. Maybe even some presents.

While we're on the topic, I think you should be able to register for gifts at Bed Bath & Beyond or Target or Best Buy for your fiftieth birthday. Registering for gifts is the most decadent, self-indulgent, brilliant idea ever devised—so why is it limited to the newly engaged? It's beyond me why all those little scanner guns are reserved for brides- and grooms-to-be when the real buying power is with the baby boomers. Seriously, think about it. Registering for gifts for a fiftieth-birthday party is the best idea since Diet Rite Cola (the first diet soda, also fifty).

You're welcome, fellow boomers.

The Big Day

Thursday: Four Days Before the Big Day

This morning my eyes popped open at 5:45 AM and I couldn't get back to sleep. Turns out, I'm getting pretty excited about this upcoming milestone. I think I'm having a party or something. My husband has been all secrets and sly grins for the last month and a half, and Annie no less so. Something is going on, but I don't have any details. And frankly, I don't want any. It's taken a while, but suddenly I'm excited.

I left work at 1:00 PM because of an appointment, but also because I am taking both Friday and Monday off, so why not go home early to prepare? After my appointment, I came home and "worked" anyway, catching up on the dozens of emails I got in between the time I left the office and the time I got home. I have five student programs in various stages of completion. There are teachers to hire, supplies to get, presenters to book—but after I finished with those emails, I was done. For the next few days, I am the Birthday Girl. In honor of that, I popped open a bottle of champagne.

Last night, I didn't get home from work until about six forty-five. My youngest, Christopher, was home from school—sick, coughing, miserable, tired but unable to sleep, hungry but unable to eat. My husband, Angelo, was there, too. But I walked straight past them into the dining room when I came in the door, because a glance through the dining room window on my walk up the driveway had told me that someone had lit a candle and placed what looked like a wrapped flower on the table. I went in to see what was up. Presents? *Already?* There was, in fact, a single rose in a vase. Propped up against it was an envelope. Inside the envelope, on the front of the card, was a dark ocean with an ominous black fin slicing through the water. When I opened the card, the first notes of a familiar movie theme sounded: *dun-dunh, dun-dunh, dun-dunh, dun-dunh.* "You know it's coming . . . ," the card warned.

I know it is. I can't wait.

Friday: Three Days Before the Big Day

My first day off as Birthday Girl, and I went to work. All I needed to do was go to a school and meet a teacher who was joining one of my programs, but it was work nevertheless. It was a quick trip to and from, so I was done by 10:30 AM. I drove back home to pick up Christopher, and we headed to the Southeast train station in Brewster, New York, to pick up Annie. Let the festivities begin!

And they did. We started at lunch. We went to a place we used to go to during my single-parent days, back when Annie and Christopher were little and we knew the manager and it was always crowded and fun: Señor Pancho's, the Mexican restaurant that arrived in Connecticut about twenty years ago, helping out us transplanted Texans just a little bit by offering beans and rice, jalapeños in every dish, and margaritas (at Connecticut prices, however). When we got to the restaurant today, we were the only ones there. More attention for us! We ordered drinks and quesadillas and ate chips and got the party started.

By this evening, however, accompanying Annie on a last-minute trip to Target, I suddenly felt overwhelmed. Deliciously and excitedly overwhelmed, but overwhelmed just the same. I texted Angelo from the car and told him I couldn't believe how much they are all doing for me. That he must be exhausted. He texted back, "I'm in bed already." Resting up for tomorrow, no doubt.

Saturday: Two Days Before the Big Day

The day of the big—something. I am choosing to get off the grid. Unplug. Disconnect. Sign off. Just for today, though, because tomorrow I have some birthday partying to do . . . I think.

Sunday: One Day Before the Big Day

So, yes, there was a party. A big one. A wonderful one. But before the party there was lunch at the Black Rock Tavern for the family. Family I didn't even expect to be there—Antonio and Marilyn up from Pelham, Victor and Lina up from Chappaqua, Susie and Stephan here from Middletown, and Christina, Tony's sister, in from New Paltz. It turns out my husband and my daughter can be quite the little party planners. And secret-keepers, too.

After a late lunch, we all came back to the house. Annie and Angelo had been moving stuff and cleaning the whole evening before, so it was obvious that something was up, but I never expected so much. Friends and neighbors showed up bearing gifts. There was a ton of food—good food—and, to top it off, an enormous, choc-olate-mocha ganache birthday cake with the requisite number of candles, which I managed to mostly blow out. If I'd remembered to make a wish, it would have been something along the lines of *I wish I could have a party at my house, with tons of food and an enormous chocolate-mocha ganache cake, to which all my family and friends were invited.* As it turns out, I didn't have to make that wish for it to come true.

Age and wine are not the best combination for remembering stuff. Add the exhilaration I was experiencing, and any significant or poignant moments that happened last night lost their chance of being etched in my memory. But here's what I do remember: I've never felt so grateful or loved or blessed in my life. Angelo, Annie, Christopher, and Annie's boyfriend, Tony, took care of everything. Everything. Every single person's presence at my house on Saturday night contributed to my experiencing a feeling I've never had before—a euphoric confidence, a certainty that I was just where I needed to be. On Saturday night I felt free of all the mundane chains of responsibility and was able to laugh and talk—and, toward the end of the evening, dance—as if none of the daily trials and tribulations of life existed. But I'm glad I don't feel that way all the time. The other stuff needs to exist, too, I think, in order for life to move forward. It's a motivator, all that irritating responsibility. It gets things done. When it was my turn in the spotlight, though—when *I* was the thing needing to get done—it was exceptional. It's a gift in itself to be celebrated. Yes, it's good to be the queen . . . at least for one night.

Monday: The Big Day

February 11. A birthday I share with Thomas Edison, Jennifer Aniston, Burt Reynolds, and Manuel Noriega. After the last four days of celebrating, I feel content upon reaching this milestone birthday properly, with enough attention to make it unforgettable (as much as is possible for me at this age) and enough time for reflection that I'm comfortable with it.

I got up at 10:30 AM today and spent the day sampling leftover hors d'oeuvres, doing a little writing, and circling, in awe, the mound of presents I've received, not ready to disturb the astonishing pile of good wishes. It's not that I was completely uncomfortable with turning fifty. It just didn't seem possible that I could have reached this "golden" age without something more—more achievement, more wisdom, more money. But so it goes. Here I am, and that in itself is an achievement. I'm happy to be here—still fighting the same battles I did when I was forty-nine or even thirty-nine, perhaps, but here all the same. Everybody has a "fifty" story—those who got here, anyway. I'm happy that when someone tells me they're celebrating their fiftieth birthday this year, I'll be able to respond by saying, "Oh, it's not so bad. Mine was perfect."

The C-Word

You know what there are a lot of commercials for on daytime TV? Food. Fast food, healthy food, snack food, good food, and bad food. You know how I know this despite the fact that I am neither a stay-at-home mom nor independently wealthy? Because I turned fifty, and turning fifty is an entrée through a golden door to all manner of wonderful things—a goodie bag of new attitudes, discounts, and medical procedures.

The attitude is awesome: *I'm fifty and I'm not going to take this [expletive of choice] anymore.* It really changes one's outlook. The discounts are quite welcome, too. I get ten percent off my order on Tuesdays at my local market. And then there are the medical procedures. At a regular checkup with my doctor long before I got my first AARP magazine, he wrote on a prescription pad, "Colonoscopy" and added verbally, "You should get one," like he was advising me to start an IRA or something.

I took the little piece of gray paper, tucked it into my purse, smiled, said, "See you next year," and promptly forgot about it. Until a couple of weeks later, that is, when my husband said one night, "You know, I never did get a colonoscopy, I should probably think about getting one." This is the kind of romantic talk we indulge in now that our kids are gone.

I responded by running to my purse to retrieve that same little piece of gray paper that held the name of a local gastroenterologist.

"We should get one together!" he said when I showed it to him. See? Crazy like teenagers, we are.

So I said, "Sure, go ahead and make all the arrangements." I figured I was safe that way, since he'd never remember to do it.

A week later, however, my husband had all the facts on the prescribed procedure. The first fact was, we couldn't do it together. To this day, I'm not sure if I was happy or disappointed about that. So he scheduled our procedures three weeks apart, and he was going first. The second piece of news: we needed to block out at least two days to have this thing done. (That's where the extended television-commercial watching comes in.) The third: each of us would need the other as a driver afterward. Because of the debilitating humiliation, I supposed—but no, it was because of the sedation. Sedation? This procedure might be manageable after all!

You don't realize how many references to the posterior and its functions people make throughout the day until you've scheduled a colonoscopy. Once you do, sit back and marvel at the eruption of expressions that ensue. On the day before, during the prep, one might comment, "This is a pain in the ass!" and then smile at the accuracy of the remark. Later that evening, after not having had anything but a liquid diet all day, you might find the observation "This diet is full of crap" escaping your lips and hear your spouse groan at the fact that this is the fifteenth procedure-appropriate comment you've made that day. It will happen. You'll see.

And now the moment you've all been waiting for: the colonoscopy. Here's exactly what it was like: I got to the outpatient surgical center. I put on a gown. I lay down on a gurney. The nice gastroenterologist came and talked to me, and then the smiling anesthesiologist came and talked to me. I put on my little blue shower cap and was wheeled by friendly nurses into the "treatment room." There was a small whiteboard on the wall that said WELCOME, CYNTHIA EASTMAN!

"Oh, how nice," I said.

Then the smiling anesthesiologist said, "I'm going to put this mask on you; then I'll inject this into your IV line . . . " and then I was out.

Forty-five minutes later, I came to in the same little cubicle in which I'd started out. I was pleasantly sleepy and not uncomfortable at all. My husband came in a few minutes later and said . . . something. Then the nice gastroenterologist came in and said I had a good-looking colon and that I'd won the best-prep-of-the-day gold star. One of the friendly nurses brought me buttered toast and tea. After about twenty minutes of this dreaminess, I got my comfy clothes back on and was escorted out to the car, which my husband helpfully drove up to the door so as not to put too much pressure on my navigational skills. (Sedation, remember?) As we drove home, my husband said . . . something. When I got home, I had a chicken salad sandwich and it was about the best chicken salad sandwich I've ever had in my life. Then I took a nap.

I tell you all this because colonoscopies are one of the best preventative procedures you can take to effectively combat colon cancer. They are recommended at fifty, but the number of people I know who are over fifty and haven't had one is . . . well, somewhere around fifty. My husband—who, by the way, experienced just as easy a time as I did, removal of a benign, mushroom-size polyp notwithstanding—was one of those until we finally planned to do it together. It takes a day and a half at the most (though I suppose it could be a full two days if you played your cards right). And not eating for a day or so isn't horrible. Really. Put it in perspective. It could save your life.

So here's the moral of the story: go do it.
Now.

My Education

Fifty does funny things to people. For one thing, it makes people decide not to take as much crap about stuff anymore. One day you're forty-nine, taking a bunch of crap, and then the next day you're fifty and you're not going to take it anymore. You get to say things like, "I'm too old for this," and people kind of look at you and go, "Yeah, you're right."

Given that, I've had a little black cloud following me around for most of my life, and now that I'm in my fifties, I'm finally going to dispel it once and for all. It's a cloud that probably started forming early on, though because my childhood was a brightly lit place of cutting through backyards, swimming in the neighborhood pool, climbing trees, and riding bikes, I likely didn't notice it. In my recollections of my younger years, I am always wearing shorts and a T-shirt and I'm running. The sky is blue and clear—no black clouds visible.

As I grew older, however, the black cloud of What People Think of Me began to form. As I advanced through school, I began to realize that people form opinions of you based on whom you hang out with or where you live or what kind of car you drive, and I became a magnet for the black-cloud particles that came with worrying about those opinions. I don't think anyone else could see them, but maybe they sensed them.

In any case, the low self-esteem that black cloud represented began early on, and it shaded my perception of myself and influenced the decisions I made. Like when I fell wildly in love and thought it was a good idea to quit school and get married. It wasn't important to me at the time to continue on with my eclectic, crazy-quilt major. Should I be an actress? A teacher? A social worker? A journalist? A Swedish translator? These were all career decisions I contemplated in the two and a half years I was in college in Austin, Texas. Fortunately, I didn't have to figure it out. Within six months of my dropping out, I was married and managing a Hallmark Crown shop, happily straightening stacks of syrupy sentiment for $700 a month.

Fast-forward a couple of years: I am divorced, ostracized by my friends, raising two little kids all by myself. Talk about your black clouds. I walked around underneath a veritable thunderhead back in those days. I felt I'd made the decision to take care of my kids and myself in the best way I knew how, but I wasn't getting a lot of positive feedback. And when I started looking around for work, I started to feel as though my not having finished my degree was going to be a problem. I looked into programs at the University of Connecticut and some of the other close-by colleges and universities in the state (they're all close by—it's Connecticut; you can practically spit from one end to the other), but none of them fit my lifestyle. "Lifestyle" meaning I worked all day, took care of kids the rest of the time, and slept a few hours in between. Colleges and universities are funny, too—they want a ton of money to educate you. I didn't have a ton of money; in fact, I barely had an ounce. So the pursuing-higher-education thing wasn't really looking like an option for me. I had to work, but I was going to have to do so without obtaining a degree.

I went to work for the local school district as a paraprofessional. Although none of us was trained in any way, most of my colleagues had a four-year degree, and my lack of formal education often made me feel as though I wasn't as good as they were—usually because those in a position of authority made me feel that way. When I say they "made" me feel that way, I know I have to own up to some responsibility for allowing them to do so. And here is what this little exercise is about: I am now throwing off the mantle of inadequacy. I am adequate. I'm more than adequate. I am, at times, exemplary.

It occurs to me that if I had heard about a woman who, after getting a divorce, continued to work while raising her two kids as a single parent and completed a master's degree in education, I would be impressed. I would sit with this woman over a cup of coffee and applaud her efforts to do something for herself while she continued to take care of her family. I would probably make sympathetic noises at the hard parts and ooh and aah at the dramatic parts. I would take my leave thinking, *Wow, she really did a good job!*

But do I give myself the same pat on the back that I would give to this fictional stranger? No. But I should. I am nontraditionally educated, but I am educated. It's true I don't have a bachelor's degree, but I'm also certain that the degree I would have earned over thirty years ago had I not dropped out would have done little to prepare me for the work I am currently doing.

When I chose to go into my master's program, I knew that without a bachelor's degree, the state of Connecticut wouldn't certify me as a teacher, but I chose to do it anyway. I can't get a job in a school district as a teacher or even at the Connecticut State Department of Education without that certification, but you know what? I don't care anymore. I think there's something to this turning-fifty thing, because I am finding that my new perspective is something along the lines of: judge me on my demonstrated abilities and merit, and not on what I should have done over thirty years ago. This is not to minimize all those people who take the traditional path and earn traditional degrees. Bully for them. But this is about me—this is about taking a giant step out from under my little black you-should-have-finished-your-degree cloud and taking pride in my achievements. I've worked hard at all my jobs, and I've left the places where I've worked better than when I arrived. And I didn't learn how to do that at college.

Thanks, Life.

Pets as Children

Some new friends invited my husband and me over to have a glass of wine. After a quick tour of their home, we settled in on the sun porch with several platters of tasty cheese, veggies, and bread and several glasses of wine. Our hostess took the wicker love seat—by herself, because one of the two cats they own was asleep on it, taking up half the cushion. That was okay; there was plenty of seating left. Naturally, after we took the obligatory toll of who has how many kids and where they all are, we got to the more important discussion: How cute are our cats? We talked about other stuff, too: travel, work, family. But clearly the cats—especially because eventually cat number two showed up to say hello to company—were the center of attention.

I am not quite sure when this happened, this pets-as-children thing. It's not like we carry pictures of our cat around with us—but do we earnestly join the funny-things-our-cat-does conversation? We most certainly do. I think it might have happened slowly and insidiously over the last couple of years. For the most part, all of our kids have gone their separate ways. They come back and visit—and sometimes briefly take up residence—but the separation has occurred in all three: they no longer need us as parents on a daily basis.

There we were in an empty nest, with no more parental duties save the occasional distress call, and then we got Maia—who, as a cat, is pretty independent. She no more needs us than she needs a little yellow kitty slicker to go out in the rain, but she tolerates us because of our ability to buy food and open it for her. But it's starting to look like *we* might need *her*. My husband will call me insistently into the living room from the kitchen, and when I get in there he's not asking me to help lift the sofa off his leg; he's saying, "Look how she's sleeping—isn't she adorable?" Like she's a baby three days home from the hospital. Ridiculous.

But even more ridiculous is the behavior I recently found myself guilty of. Since our cat is so much smarter than the other cats on the block (shh—the neighbors think theirs is), I thought I'd try a little training experiment: I put all her toys in a basket on the floor to see if she would return them when she was done playing with them. She always brings one of her toys upstairs when she comes up to bed with us and leaves it on the floor as if to have it available when she wakes up. Adorable. So I thought I'd give her her own basket—to keep things organized. Whenever I saw the stuffed fish or fake leopard-skin mouse around the house, I'd pick them up and put them back in the basket. You know, to teach her.

One morning, I came downstairs and found the fish and the leopard-skin mouse on the stairs, and the new purple mouse under the table in the dining room. I gathered all three and headed toward the living room to put them back—and that's when it hit me. Someone *was* being trained to put all the toys back in the basket, but it wasn't the cat. On the contrary, she was leaving her toys around more frequently, and in new and different places, for *me* to find and return!

How funny is she?

Wait till I tell the neighbors.

Best-Laid Plans

Right before I left my job as a professional development special-ist (it sounds more exciting than it was), I emailed my fellow educators and colleagues to notify them about my plans, such as they were. One of the teachers I worked with, a woman named Barbara, contacted me soon after my departure and asked if we could meet. She needed advice, she said—she had recently been "encouraged" by her school district to take a retirement package to help the district out with its ongoing budget issues (she wasn't the only one; there were over seventy such packages offered to district employees). She wanted to see how I was doing after leaving my job and wondered if I could be of any help to her as she contemplated a similar fate.

Being the helpful Pollyanna type, I agreed to meet with Barbara, but for the week or so beforehand, I fretted about what in the heck I'd be able to do for her. I hadn't really done anything new since I'd left my position, despite marginal attempts otherwise, and I felt ill-prepared and empty-handed when the time came for us to meet. But I went anyway. There was wine on the agenda.

But wait a minute—let me make a short story long. The day I was to meet with Barbara was the day before my fifty-first birthday. And I have to say, there's something very liberating about anticipat-ing one's fifty-first birthday. There is hardly any stress at all about the wonderful things one's family members are planning; you can just order a pizza and watch *Lost* without any worry that a big sur-prise party is being planned. You can also finally stop noticing all the other people and things turning fifty, and you have none of the fear of receiving any of the ridiculous and sometimes unflattering "You're fifty!" birthday cards that some people just can't seem to resist. Yes, it's a nice time indeed. You can plan a meeting for which you are totally unprepared without experiencing any additional anxiety. So I packed up my vacant calendar and the brochures I'd made for my Writing and Multiculturalism programs, which I had yet to send out or market in the slightest, and drove to Danbury to meet Barbara.

After a quick catch-up about family and friends, I let her start the conversation, since I had no idea what to lead with. And she began to talk—mostly about her apprehension about leaving a career in which she had just spent thirty years, and her unfamiliarity with how in the world she should proceed. Then it was my turn. I started telling her about my decision to leave a salaried, benefit-providing job in what would turn out to be a monstrous economic downturn. I had, from out of the blue, been offered a part-time teaching posi-tion that helped out, but mostly I was just out of work. I'd taken on a volunteer position at the town library to run a student program and was helping out my husband in his visitation practice, but I hadn't done any of the ADL presentations I had trained for in July, I hadn't contacted any schools about doing professional-development work-shops, and I hadn't applied for any other salaried, benefit-providing jobs. And to be honest, I told her, I was literally down to my last twenty bucks—though that wasn't as bad as it seemed, since my teaching paychecks would kick back in at the end of the week.

No, I had to admit, I hadn't done any real planning for this gig. My husband and I had known that it would be tight and that it might be some time before I began doing the kind of work that I really wanted to do, but as far as planning for it went—nope, nothing. And the result was . . . awesome. The work I was doing was work that I was good at and that I wanted to do. I'd had time to shake off any of the lingering stress from my last job, and to be in a position to feel good about myself when I did finally go and interview for all those jobs I hadn't applied for yet.

The more I talked to Barbara, the more I realized that I was, in fact, in a pretty good place. Sure, I had no consistent income, but neither did I have off-the-charts stress levels or the constant feeling that I wasn't doing the best job that I could do. I don't know how Barbara felt after our meeting, but I left feeling pretty good about my choices in the preceding year or so—and I think she left feeling a little better about her prospects, too.

The really nice thing about being fifty-something is that I can look around at the places I've been, look back down the road I've traveled, and be pretty okay with it all. I am grateful that I can get up each morning somewhat achy but still able to plant both feet on the floor and greet a brand-new day. When I met Barbara that day, as I ruminated about where I was in my life, I realized that it was true that I'd been there before—but I hadn't been *this* me there before. And this me, the fifty-one-year-old model, could deal with it. I had a little more maturity (okay, a lot more maturity), a little more confidence, and the tiniest bit more wisdom. But not all the wisdom. I'm definitely still working on that one.

Gotta/Wanna

My laundry basket sat piled high in the middle of my room. Overpiled, in fact, if that's a word. And it was only *one* of my laundry baskets, as the one full of my husband's clothes was down by the laundry chute in the kitchen, and the one full of towels and sheets was in the office. It's possible that I had scattered them around the house so they would feel less threatening, but more than likely it was the result of an episode of MB (menopause brain).

Why was there so much laundry to do? Because doing laundry was not just a matter of finding the scattered baskets and hauling them down to the washing machine. It required my taking the baskets, the detergent, and the softener to the car and driving down to the local Laundromat. And that, my friends, was not fun.

There was way too much snow out there. On my car, in my car, in my driveway, on the roads, in the parking lots—everywhere. Which meant it was cold. And possibly icy. I barely have enough coordination to traverse the driveway and get into the car without a mishap. I was supposed to juggle loads of laundry and laundry accessories as well? And a book? (I certainly wasn't going to the Laundromat without a book.)

No, this was not an acceptable activity for a woman in her (early) fifties. I had a fireplace that worked and a perfectly acceptable sofa right in front of it. Why would I want to lug two weeks' worth of laundry out my door and over to a grayish, ill-lit establishment with plastic chairs? That's easy: I didn't. As I get older, I'm finding that making the decisions about what I've "gotta" do and what I "wanna" do is coming much more easily. There is no doubt that I gotta do the laundry. But did I wanna? Nope. Not if it meant the acrobatics described above. I still had a couple of sets of sheets, my husband had a few more clean shirts, and my black tights never show the dirt. Laundry becomes dire only when the availability of clean underwear is at stake, and, happily, it wasn't dire yet.

There was a time in my life when I would have felt guilty making the decision not to do the laundry. And not only *not* do the laundry, but stay home and read in front of the fire instead. But now I've reached an age where I have a little more confidence in my ability to prioritize and a little more wisdom about what's important in life. Reading a good book in front of the fire? Important. Risking life and limb for clean towels? Not important.

I've gotta see about that fire . . .

Family

ENS
(Empty-Nest Syndrome)

So, they're all gone. The doors to their rooms are closed. The quilts are as flat on the beds now as they were two months ago after the last one left. No rumples from balled-up pajamas, no dents from books or CD cases, no piles of magazines, no piles of clothes. We've finally run out of plastic shopping bags, owing to the infrequency of our trips to the grocery store. And we have less food—a lot less food. So this is what it's like. I've heard about empty-nest syndrome, of course, but here it finally is. Hallelujah!

Not that I don't dearly love each of my darling children. I do. I am lucky to have had such wonderful human beings in my life every single blessed day for the last twenty-four years. Annie, the eldest, went off to California to mine for career gold like a forty-niner. Justine's path took her to Arizona and grad school. Christopher, my baby, was the last one out of the nest and headed to Boston to go to college. How proud I am of them. How amazing they are. How nice that they are gone!

I had some indication of how this time might look before they left. While the girls were at school, they were gone for weeks at a time, sometimes for a whole summer. Chris spent a few summers in Maine with my parents, where he worked at the local ice-cream stand. These were trial periods for us, a chance to experience a child-free home. They were gone, but not really, because there was still the occasional phone call or weekend visit home. In June, as if to remind us of what we'd be missing, they all came home. All three were there 24-7, parking their cars in our driveway, watching TV, working—sometimes—and needing special foods (or just *more* food). It was a large, loud, chaotic, familial summer camp. I was the counselor, and Angelo was the director—which meant he stayed in the office upstairs, issuing memos on appropriate behavior ("I really think a curfew should be enforced"). I, meanwhile, managed the day-to-day activities ("Okay, kids, time for the weenie roast!").

Then, in September, they were gone.

The first week after they left, I couldn't go straight home from work. The Rite Aid drugstore held an almost magnetic draw for me; I kept discovering that I "needed" to buy various hair products and office supplies before turning into our now-empty driveway. The brain acuity I'd needed to mentally, almost psychically, keep track of each child's whereabouts for the past few months was no longer necessary.

So I became stupid. I couldn't process the simplest bit of information without hours of concentration.

"Do you want to rent a movie tonight, Cindy?"

"What? Why are you tormenting me with these riddles?"

Time held no meaning. I didn't need to be home at a certain hour to fix meals, provide transportation, or just be there. I wasn't necessary for anything. Maybe the cat still needed me to feed her and let her out, but she could wait, and wait . . . and wait.

Once, a very long time ago, I read a submission to the "Life in These United States" section of *Reader's Digest*. I must have been only about twelve, but I remember it to this day. It went something like this: The wife and husband stand on the front porch, watching their last child drive off to college. The wife turns to the husband and says wistfully, "Well, hon, you're all I've got left." The husband turns back to the wife and says, "Hon, I'm all you started with."

God knows why that anecdote stuck with me, especially since it didn't mean anything to me at age twelve, but I've remembered it ever since. The difference for me is that the husband I have now isn't the one I started out with pre-children. We met mid-children. We became a family when my daughter and his daughter were sixteen and my son was eleven. Our empty nest is a first-time experience for us. We met and negotiated and blended more than ten years ago, and our relationship grew only after soccer practices, chorus, college visits, and visitation schedules.

Then, suddenly, we were all we had. And it was a little dicey there for a couple of weeks. To be honest, Angelo became as stupid as I did. It took time for us to adjust to just being with each other without all those distractions. Anything we wanted to impart had better have been imparted, because now it's time to watch as our children move forward with their own lives. And here we are—all alone in our empty nest, without the ties of children to bind us together.

Did I mention hallelujah?

When Chickens Come Home

"The chickens have come home to roost"—i.e., the consequences of earlier actions are making themselves felt.

In the spring of 2006, when Christopher was nineteen, I took him to the airport to fly to California. He was going to join Annie, then twenty-five, to help her move back across the country. She and her boyfriend, Tony, had decided that while California sure was pretty, it wasn't the place for them. Not when both their families lived back East. I was in complete agreement.

So Chris went to Los Angeles and arrived in time to help Annie pack. They FedExed seventeen boxes to their dad's house and engineered the rest of her stuff into her car. Chris, as it turned out, was a packing genius. He was available to exhibit this skill because he was taking a semester off from school and had yet to find gainful employment. Fortunately, he was living at home, so there weren't any bills to pay. (Well, actually, there were—he just wasn't the one paying them.) He is not a kid who isn't willing to work; it's just that he, like Annie, was in search of the perfect job, even if it was only a temporary one, something to do until he decided where and/or when to go back to school. Faced with the challenge out in California, he came to life and became invaluable to Annie and Tony during the packing and moving process. Tony was flying back to start a new job, so I was secretly glad Chris was there; he would be along for the ride, so Annie wouldn't be alone.

Not that she couldn't do it alone. Three years earlier, she'd done just that. She wanted to spend the summer in L.A.; she had a car; what was stopping her? Not much, as it turned out. She found some old school friends who were up to the adventure—for the first couple of hundred miles, anyway. After that, however, they had to go back to their jobs, so she dropped them off at an airport some-where around Tennessee and kept on driving. She'd spent the week-end in Maine just before she left, so by the end of the week she had driven literally from one end of the country to the other. Her phone calls along the way were memorable. She was in awe of the land-scape and the size of the country. She was also a little alarmed at the behavior of some of the truck-stop habitués.

Now, three years later, she was heading back east, accompanied by her brother. My two children, on the other side of the country, in a car jammed with the combined households of Annie and Tony's California living: a huge television set, a DVD player, a PlayStation, a VCR, a TiVo, and some clothes and towels. All heading home. My heart was in my throat the whole time. The first phone call was a little nerve-racking: Annie was stressed, and Chris, I think, was asleep. But as the trip wore on, the phone calls were filled with pri-vate jokes, laughter, and vivid descriptions of the scenery and char-acters they were driving by.

And then they were home. Tired and hungry and in need of a shower, but still laughing about private road-trip jokes that only they shared. For over a month, they were both home again, Christopher still without a job, and Annie looking for work in New York City. Tony was already a month into his job, and they had already found an apartment, so it was only a matter of time until she left again. Like her brother, she was hoping for the perfect job, but she was reasonable enough to know that she needed to work so she could join Tony in the city and start living her life. Once she left and the clothes and the boxes were gone, I knew it would be much quieter around the house. Chris would still be here, but he doesn't really make much noise—plus, he would be on his way soon, too, because he didn't want to live in our basement forever. At least, I didn't think he did.

I am a big fan of Cesar Millan, the Dog Whisperer. In one episode, he encouraged a woman who finally gained mastery over her dog's errant behavior to take pride in what she'd done. If you put positive energy out there, he said, the universe incorporates the energy, and everyone—even the dog—can feel it.

I am not one to take credit for my children. They are a gift to me; I've always felt that way. But after I heard Cesar tell that woman to take pride in her accomplishment, I decided it would be okay for me to take just a little pride in how I raised my children. Christopher's going out to California, and Annie's letting him, is just one example of how they look out for each other. They are strong and competent, conscientious and compassionate. The pride I feel for them is just bristling with positive energy, and I'd be doing the universe a favor by sharing this energy. So, from here on out, I'm saying it out loud: I am proud of my kids. They grew into wonderful adults, and if I had a tiny bit to do with it, then I am happy to own up to it.

Open Heart

One day, I was sitting in the library of a school where I was providing professional development in technology integration to teachers. I was scheduled to be there until the end of the day, but at 2:00 PM on a Friday afternoon, no one wants to spend an hour in a consultation about ingenious ways to integrate technology into their curriculum. So I was using my free time to organize my notes, catch up on my to-do list, and clean out my email—and then my cell phone rang.

Finally, I thought. I had been expecting a call from my mom all afternoon to see how her test had gone. After months and months of tests, she was getting a catheterization to prove once and for all that nothing was wrong.

"They're admitting me," she said when I answered. And for whatever reason, I started to cry.

"What?" I said, wiping the streams of tears from my face.

"They found a blockage, so they are doing bypass surgery tomorrow morning."

"What?" I repeated intelligently, rooting around the librarian's desk for a box of tissues. In my head, I was thinking, *How can my mother be telling me all this in such a calm manner? Why am I crying and she isn't? Where is my dad? Why in hell is the custodian walking in here now, while I'm crying, and why am I using a pink index card to blow my nose?*

I gathered my emotions together. "Huh?" Another intelligent response.

"I am going to be admitted now, and they will perform the surgery tomorrow morning," my mother continued. "Don't worry—everything is all right. Dad is here, and he's going to stay with me."

I continued to draw on my unknown reserve of emotional strength. "What?" I whined. "Should I come down?"

And my mom, who continues to be my mother in the face of all sorts of trials and tribulations, told me, "No."

So I dried my eyes, shut down my computer, shoved my paperwork into my bag, smiled apologetically at the custodian for still being there, and for crying, and went out to my car. Once there, I pushed the speed-dial button to get my husband's cell phone.

"My mom has to have open-heart surgery. She's having it tomorrow. I should be there. I don't know what the doctor said. I guess he's good. I don't know when the surgery is. I should go down. I'm still at the school—"

"Go home," he interrupted me. "Relax. I'll be home soon."

Open. Heart. Surgery. Two of the words, I can deal with. It's the last one that causes a problem. Oh, we have all had surgery of some kind—C-sections, hysterectomies, oral, minor—but this one, *open-heart surgery* . . . it's too much to deal with. And yet we will have to deal with it, because it is tomorrow.

The next day, while my mother was under the knife, I went to the gym. My husband and I had just joined a week earlier to finally address the annoying, creeping weight gain we were both finding such a nuisance. With the membership came a consultation with a trainer; my turn was on Saturday morning at nine, an hour after the surgery was to begin.

I stated my disclaimer immediately upon arrival. "I might be a little distracted. My mother is in surgery at this moment."

The trainer asked if I'd like to put off the session so I could go be with her.

"Well, she's in Florida, so no, that's okay," I said. But for the rest of the day, I wondered, *Should I be there?*

Later, freshly exercised and properly trained, I bought a pack of cigarettes. I'd quit two years earlier but still smoked sporadically, depending on whose corrupting influence I was under. As a nod to my nonsmoking status, I threw away half of the cigarettes when I got home; then I smoked and smoked on the back porch until my husband got home from the class he teaches on Saturdays. My mother smoked forever: while she was pregnant, during our childhood, in the car. Her mother smoked Camel non-filters until the day she died (not from a smoking-related illness, surprisingly enough—she simply went to bed one night and died, just like that). But as I sat there and smoked, I thought to myself, *How stupid am I? My mom is undergoing bypass surgery, and here I sit, lighting up. Dumb.* Or scared.

The rest of the day was a blur until I finally got the call: "She's out. She's fine."

On Sunday we learned that it wasn't a single bypass, or even a triple, as previously reported—it was a quadruple freaking bypass. Four! Like Bill Clinton! They used leg and mammary veins to do it.

When I finally talked to my mother on Sunday, she was feeling no pain. "Yep, I'm fine. Don't worry. There are plenty of people to help out. Don't come down. We're fine!"

But still I wondered: *Should I be there?* By this time I had spoken to my brother and sister. We connect with support and emotion. We do that. I am the oldest, so I made all the calls. It was my brother's job to allay my fears. My sister is the youngest; with her, I talked about how we couldn't believe this was happening. But we were all in touch; we were all vigilant. And we knew that my mother's heart was stronger than any knife or procedure. Her heart was what had given us the bond we had with one another.

By Sunday night, my resolve was almost complete. I needed to be there. I *would* be there. The next morning, I spoke to my boss about missing the week at work. Even if it wasn't okay with her, I would go, but I was confident that she would understand and would probably, in fact, make me go. And she did. So I made my reservations that morning, and then I went home to pack.

By Wednesday morning, I was on a plane to Tampa. My dad picked me up with his friend Mr. Taylor. He doesn't drive much anymore, so he relies on others for rides to his various commitments and activities—usually my mom, but since she was indisposed, he had made other arrangements. We made mostly small talk during the hour-long trip to Sarasota.

We went straight to the hospital. When we got to my mother's room, I walked in, saw her, and began to cry—again. Not because she looked frail or sick or anything. The woman looked fabulous, complete with freshly applied lipstick. But seeing my parent sitting in a hospital gown and knowing that a four-hour, invasive surgery had just been performed on her most delicate and essential organ—her heart—brought on a tumultuous emotional attack.

There is no question that the heart is the most important organ, and that it is important to every living thing—well, every one that relies on a heart to live, anyway. But unless you are a medical student specializing in cardiology, when we refer to the heart, we're not talking about the organ. We typically use it in an emotional sense or, at the very least, as a way of describing someone's spirit, courage, or strength. And this is what I am finally getting around to saying: my mother's heart is the last thing I would expect would need surgery. The definition for "open heart," if it were in the dictionary (not a medical one), would have a picture of my mother next to it. She is "open heart" personified. To know that someone had cut into her chest and rerouted the passage of her heart's function is something I just couldn't get my head around. There couldn't be anything wrong with her heart. Maybe her knees or eyes. Maybe. But her heart? Nah. Not possible. This heart is full of love and Jesus and the homeless, and children and friends and poetry. This heart knows its mission: to love without reason, to give without limit. This heart beats strong and loud, and we all heard it—we, her family, her friends, and even strangers, who were the recipients of its bounty. How could it be sick?

The home health aide assigned to ensure that my mother could send the little yellow balls floating to the top of the plastic breathing contraption—like she was playing some sort of freakish lung-capacity lottery—praised my mother's healing abilities to the high heavens. "I've never seen anyone heal so quickly," she declared. She wasn't exaggerating: my mother's six-inch-long incision practically disappeared before our eyes. It seemed someone wanted to make sure her newly mended heart was properly protected.

My week in Florida flew by too quickly. Tons of friends stopped by, called, dropped off meals. On Valentine's Day, I flew home. And, not surprisingly, I had with me for the flight a Valentine's Day present from my mother. Wrapped in white tissue paper, it was a small package of chocolates, a bookmark with an inspirational quote, and a travel relaxation kit for my tired eyes. The white tissue paper was decorated in tiny red hearts, hand-drawn in red marker by my mother. There was nothing wrong with that heart. No way.

Found Time

Every once in a while, a phenomenon occurs that I've heard referred to as "found time." This supposedly means that all of a sudden, a period of time that was previously booked becomes available to you. Like when a meeting is suddenly canceled and you get to go food shopping instead. Or one day you look up and there are no children in your home, and you have to figure out how to fill your days. Like that. Found time.

I've always wanted to have a drink at the Campbell Apartment. Why? Well, as it says on the red leather–bound menu, it offers "cocktails from another era." It's situated on the upper level of Grand Central Station, and it once belonged to John Campbell, leased from Cornelius Vanderbilt as a private office. Old New York always intrigues me. When I visit, I find myself imagining what it was like to walk the sidewalks a hundred years ago, speculating about what the buildings originally housed, and wondering if all the little parks were well kept and inviting. So I figured if I saved up, I could spend twenty bucks on a cocktail at the Campbell Apartment and experience life as it was at that time, just for a while.

So, as fate would have it, on a recent trip I took to New York City, my train arrived on time at Grand Central, but my daughter did not. I caught a little bit of "found time." Without a shred of guilt, I texted Annie that I would be waiting for her at The Campbell Apartment, and I walked right up to the entrance. The bar opens at 3:00 PM; I was a few minutes early. Still, there were several people ahead of me. I chalked it up to the popularity of the joint and waited for the double doors at the top of the stairs to open.

It turned out that the people waiting with me were all members of one party, and they were waiting for more. They were about to surprise a young couple who were getting engaged at that very moment. They rushed into the tiny room—big for an apartment, small for a bar—and I was left with the lone barstool at the end of the bar. I squeezed in next to a woman who was in deep conversation with another young woman, who was intent upon listing all the grad schools she had applied to (it was fascinating stuff, let me tell you). The hostess, in black cocktail dress and pearls, took pity on my plight, although she was clearly delighted about having such a windfall party so early in the day. She handed me the red leather menu and told me she would take my order herself so I wouldn't get lost in the crush of the engagement party's orders.

I read and reread the three-page menu, toying with the idea of ordering a fancy cocktail. I had the time, but the reason I'd taken the train into the city in the first place was to meet up with a friend I hadn't seen in twenty or so years—she was in town to visit her son at Columbia and cheer him on at his last football game as a senior—so I decided on a glass of California chardonnay. A benign glass of white wine was less likely to make me stumble up to Columbia and make a bad impression.

My fourteen dollar glass of wine was poured, as promised, by the lovely hostess, and I sat at the bar wondering how a twenty-first-century woman occupies herself alone at the bar. This is definitely not in my skill set. I finally did what I always do: pulled out my notebook and started to write. (I always think the other patrons and/or delightful hostesses will think I'm a famous writer—or, at the very least, a food critic—and ask me about my work or offer me something on the house. Sadly, this never happens.) I didn't have long to establish my authority with my writing, however: Annie arrived when I was halfway into my chardonnay. The hostess said she had a cozy table for two in the corner, and, as Annie had never made it to The Campbell Apartment before either, we stayed. And Annie ordered a Pimm's Cup, of course.

Where did we need to go? Well, yes, to meet my friend, but she was at a football game. This was serious found time here. I didn't feel rushed or worried or pressed or any of those other pushy feelings that make you feel like you can't enjoy exactly what you're doing at the moment you are doing it.

So there we were, ensconced in a dark corner and surrounded by overstuffed chairs and sofas, wood-paneled walls, and a smattering of Beautiful People, enjoying our cocktails. The room—and it is just *a* room—had a huge stone fireplace, and the whole place had a kind of eighteenth-century English manor/Manhattan Upper West Side *pied-à-terre* feeling to it. (Like I know what either of those places feels like, but that was my impression.)

Suddenly, the room exploded into applause and camera flashes; the happy couple had arrived. Annie and I excitedly joined in, clapping and smiling and even, curiously, crying a little. There were more than a few glances in our direction—as if to ask, *Who the heck are they?* —but we just clapped more loudly and smiled more broadly. It's fun to crash parties!

When both of our glasses were empty, I called my friend. She and her son were heading back to campus, and we could meet her there. I paid the bill, and we left to catch the subway shuttle to Times Square and head uptown. As we left The Campbell Apartment, I realized how good I felt. This found time had appeared, and I'd taken the opportunity to do something I'd always wanted to do. And I'd gotten to do it with Annie, and we'd had a blast.

Train ticket to Grand Central Station from Chappaqua, New York: eight dollars and twenty-five cents. A California chardonnay and Pimm's Cup at The Campbell Apartment (plus tip): thirty-one dollars. The ability to finally take some time for myself without feeling guilty and enjoy an absolutely wonderful time with my daughter: priceless.

Wedding-Belle Bliss

The rain was uninvited, but it crashed the party anyway. Gray clouds and pouring rain, and then a constant drizzle hovered over Bethlehem, Connecticut, for the two days of Annie and Tony's rehearsal and wedding. This meant that the rehearsal, supposed to be held outside at the Bellamy-Ferriday Garden on Friday night, was instead held in my living room. It also meant that the rehearsal dinner—already planned for my house, and for which my sister spruced up the backyard to accommodate all the people—was held in my living room, and kitchen, and dining room, and on my porch. Still, the wedding my daughter had envisioned and planned for three solid months was a beautiful event. The drizzle even played its part by acting as a natural air conditioner. Hmph!

I'm usually a pretty low-stress type of person, a go-with-the-flow, roll-with-the-punches kind of gal. I'm a problem solver; I have a background in managing student programs. All of this was brought to bear during Wedding Week. Crates were filled with supplies for decorating the tent and tables, food was ordered and picked up, multicolored pennants were sewn and sorted. I brought out my handy clipboard with miles of notes—a master to-do list with copies of permits and permission certificates clipped securely in place. Getting things done: this, I know how to do. What I didn't know how to do was let my little girl go and get married. There was so much to do and so much redoing because of the weather, however, that I didn't have the time to notice that a huge chunk of emotion was building in my heart.

The first person to arrive in town was the mother of the groom. Sue is the best person to do almost anything with, mostly because she is also a go-with-the-flow, roll-with-the-punches kind of gal. We work so nicely together, you'd think we've known each other since childhood. We get things done and we have a great time doing it. I had a class to teach soon after she arrived, so Sue just picked up where I left off and finished the last one hundred or so wedding favors: environmentally appropriate plastic bags filled with moose-shaped pasta and tied with green raffia and a wooden spoon. (We still have plenty left, so let me know if you have a hankering for moose-shaped whole-wheat pasta.) After class, I flew home, Sue jumped in the car, and we drove to Southeast Station to pick up the bride-to-be and her sister-in-law-to-be. It was on.

Over the next few days, more family arrived, more details were taken care of, and a twenty-four-hour watch on the weather commenced. The beautiful, picture-perfect New England sunny crispness was slowly evolving into foreboding gray coolness with the threat of rain. We were undaunted! The excitement was building, weaving its way through all the preparations, and nothing was getting in its way. We prepared and packed the white muslin treat bags for out-of-towners at the hotel, so each guest got one as he or she checked in, and then we spent most of Friday and all morning on Saturday decorating the tents and tables. Then it was time to get the bride and groom back to the hotel to get ready.

I went home to get dressed and ready to drive up to the garden. I was feeling an edginess that made putting on makeup . . . er, challenging. *Damn mascara—does it need to clump now?* (Let's not even talk about my hair. One of the Buffalo relatives is a hairstylist who volunteered to do Annie's hair, and when I was with her at the hotel, she asked him, "What could we do with my mom's hair?" He took one look at me, gave us an uncomfortable smile, and said nothing.) After a disappointing attempt at makeup, I scrounged around for a couple of gold barrettes I bought in 1978 and stuck them in my hair. We got to the site right on time and began greeting guests and, after making the last-minute decision to hold the ceremony outside (it was cloudy but not raining, so we decided to go for it), showing them to the garden. The big yellow school bus carrying the out-of-towners and others for whom it might not be a good idea to drive back afterward arrived. All we needed now was the bride.

Annie showed up a few minutes late, as beautiful as the day she was born. A small swell of emotion surged in my heart at the sight of her—but we had places to get to; it was almost time to begin. Did I mention I was the one who got to walk her down the aisle? It was an honor I'd been informed of a week earlier. I couldn't wait.

After I "gave her away," I took my place beside my husband, who contributed to the ceremony by reading a canticle by St. Francis in Italian. I started to tear up a little bit. I have always been a crier, and I make no bones about it: I cry. So there. But aside from a few tears here and there during the ceremony and reception, I held it together. Even during the toast I read, the emotions and tears stayed neatly tucked in. I think it was because of self-discipline—or maybe it was the corset I was wearing; I can't be sure. We spent the evening dancing to great music, eating sumptuous food, drinking lots of wine and champagne, and laughing with new family and old friends. When it was over, many people followed the brand-new Mr. and Mrs. back to the hotel to continue the celebration, but I went home. And fell right to sleep.

It wasn't until Monday morning, when I was driving back to the train station, that that chunk of emotion let loose from its tethers and surfaced. The wedding DJ had made a CD of some of the music from the reception, and when the mother-son song came on, the tears just started pouring. Why that song, I don't know; I didn't even dance to it. But that's the one that did it. I looked over at Sue and saw it had gotten to her as well. There we were, the mothers in the front seat, tears streaming down our faces, while Annie, Tony, and Christina laughed and reminisced about some going-on or another in the back. When they noticed we were crying, they became silent, and for a few minutes it seemed like we were all caught up in the magnitude of it all: of marriage, of love, of family. Then "Macho Man" began to blare from the stereo, the moment passed, and we were all talking about this person's surprise appearance on the dance floor and that person's atypical emotional declaration—and then we were at the station.

I cried as I hugged Annie before she got on the train. I cried as I hugged Tony, Christina, and Sue good-bye, too. And I cried for most of the drive home. They weren't happy tears or sad tears—they were just tears, the liquid manifestation of unfathomable love, the fluid release of unexpressed emotion. As we planned and worked and prepared for the wedding, I told myself, *I'm not going to let this get to me. What's the big deal anyway? Anyone can plan a wedding.* I wasn't going to be one of those melodramatic moms who seem to be trying to earn some sort of merit badge just because their daughter happens to be getting married.

But it turns out it *is* a big deal. It's very emotional. (I know— "Duh, Cin.") But even when you're aware of that fact, there's something that wells up inside you as you're hugging your new family and giving your child away, and it refuses to be waved away. It's huge.

It's love.

The Long and
Winding Road

I took a week off one month to go to Florida.

Wow! you're thinking. *Lucky duck. She can just take off a week to head south for some sun and fun, just like that.* But the goal of my trip wasn't to get a jump-start on my summer tan or to try and camouflage the increasing gray in my hair with a couple of spritzes (okay, half a bottle) of Sun-In hair lightener. No, there was a nobler goal in mind: to help my parents make their semiannual trek to Maine by volunteering as a relief driver. For twenty-three years or so, they made the pilgrimage by themselves: up from Florida to Maine in May, back down south in October. Back and forth, year after year, all by themselves. They used to share the driving responsibilities, but as my dad's eyesight grew compromised from diabetes complications, my mom took them all on, dispatching my dad to watch for route changes, hotel signs, and semis coming up suddenly on the right. My husband and I started offering our help about two years ago, but my mom is, in a word, stubborn.

Then I decided to be more assertive about it. Not that I didn't think she was capable of doing all the driving, but for Pete's sake, *everyone* could use another person to share driving duties with on a 1,500-mile, twenty-five-hour-long road trip. Sure, South Carolina is a snap, but you eventually have to go through New Jersey, so why not have an extra driver in the car? Previous reasons (excuses?) have been "There's not that much room in the car," or "I've done this so many times, I'll be fine," or "We have some people to visit on the way up—you'd be bored" (read: in the way). So finally, instead of asking, I went ahead and took the decision out of their hands and made the reservation to fly down. That was my first mistake.

I remember when my grandfather, Papa, my dad's father, had his driver's license taken away. He was in his late eighties, and after my grandmother died, he filled his time doing things around the mobile-home park for his neighbors. One of the things he did was deliver Meals on Wheels to the shut-ins—those people who, for one reason or another, couldn't get out and needed at least one of their daily meals brought to them. When his driver's license was taken away, my parents said, he was devastated.

I was in my late teens then, and I don't think I completely under-stood why it was so bad. Papa lived in a community where he could get almost anywhere on foot, and his son, my Uncle Bob, lived close enough that he could come pick him up for church or grocery shop-ping or whatever. Years later, I finally understood: it was the loss of independence that was so painful. His ability to drive had not only allowed him to pick up and go anywhere he wanted, it had made him continue to feel useful—my grandma wasn't around for him to tend to, but he'd been able to deliver meals to others. I carry a picture of Papa in my head from what turned out to be my last visit with him. I remember him sitting in the backseat of my Uncle Bob's car, gazing out the window, detached from the conversation around him. We got out at the park, enjoyed our picnic, and walked out to the beach, but he wasn't fully present, not like he had been.

This memory was with me as I made my way to Florida and back up through Georgia, South Carolina, North Carolina, and north-ward. I remained cognizant of the fact that I wasn't there to "take over" the driving; I was "helping." I didn't do all the driving; my mom took on the cross-Florida leg, the boring South Carolina stint, and the construction-strewn North Carolina route. I got Virginia,

Maryland, New Jersey, New York, and Connecticut (while she manned the imaginary passenger-side brake). I knew she had finally decided to relax when she offered to take the backseat position and took a nap somewhere south of Virginia. My dad, meanwhile, was a vigilant navigator—when he wasn't reading up on and selecting which seminars and activities he would participate in at the fifty-fifth Wesleyan University reunion he was helping to organize for that weekend.

When I flew to Florida, I was thinking that I was doing something helpful for my parents. And I still think I did. But the trip also gave me the opportunity to learn a little more about the people who raised me and taught me everything I know. I was helpful, sure, but we also had a good time, an easy trip, and a couple of good meals—when we stopped for meals, that is. (Apparently, stopping for meals is for sissies. We had a Costco-size bag of trail mix with us.)

Most importantly, though, the trip reminded me that life, and all it entails, is far different for a couple in their seventies than it is for a woman in her fifties. The culture is different, your expectations are different, and your sense of self draws on a whole different set of abilities and responsibilities. When you get older, any amount of "help" must feel like a little bit of your independence is being taken away—and independence is a gift not to be taken lightly, because it is the difference between having control of your own life or not. A good lesson to learn, whether one is a stubborn parent or a helpful child.

Grandmother, Grandma, Granny

I was going to be a grandma.

I'd known for couple of months, but I was sworn to secrecy. Annie and Tony wanted to wait until they were in their second trimester to announce the news. The only people who were permitted to know were the new grandparents. Not Another Soul! Or Else! So I kept my mouth shut.

Okay, I didn't.

I found myself telling strangers who wouldn't rat me out. I told the lady restocking cards at Stop & Shop (she said I was going to love it). The guy pumping gas across from me at the Shell station (he said I looked too young to be a grandma). A kid in a class I was subbing for (he just looked at me funny). I told all of our relatives in Italy when we were there, since they don't speak much English. I told the members of a committee I was on, but there were only three of them. One of them started knitting a baby blanket that very day. And I told my writing group. In my defense, my writing group consists of only one other writer—and I swore her to secrecy. She's probably the only one who actually did keep her mouth shut.

But as the second-trimester mark neared, Annie called to say she and Tony had relented about telling more people. My co-grandma, Sue, fired up her Bluetooth, and practically before I hung up with

Annie, three-quarters of Buffalo knew about the impending birth. I tried calling my brother and sister, but they didn't answer. I thought some more about whom to call, and then I remembered: I don't like to talk on the phone. I decided that since Sue was probably tying up all the cell signals in the Northeast anyway, I would write about it. I'm a writer; I write about stuff. So I posted an essay on my website. It was fun to see several of my friends post congratulatory comments, but it was even more exciting when I got a couple of cards in the mail—"Congrats on the New Baby!" This was getting fun. I began to wonder: Should I register somewhere for gifts?

There was a lot I needed to learn.

It had been a long time since there were babies in the family, and all my baby information was ancient—like I had learned it from cave drawings or read it on a papyrus scroll. Did we care about what Dr. Spock had to say anymore, or was he only a Vulcan on a starship now? When I was pregnant, I quit smoking and drinking. Done. Bring on the baggy clothes. Nowadays, though, Annie could barely walk down the street without a mask and plastic gloves. I made her a turkey sandwich one day, and she couldn't eat it. Know why? No deli meats. I'm not kidding; deli meats are potentially a risk. She lives in New York City, not the mountains of Afghanistan. But there are thousands of articles on millions of websites that warn against this hazardous food and that toxic ingredient. Danger lurks on every grocery shelf. I'm glad I didn't have the Internet when I was pregnant.

Here's something else: I was pretty sure that the first critical decision I would face was what I would be called. Grandma and Papa are *my* parents. I thought about going Italian—Nonna—but Sue claimed Nonna right off the bat. She's Sicilian; I wasn't going to cross her.

So I had to find just the right name. I definitely wasn't going to let the bundle of joy choose the name—that's how you end up with something like Gurcky. All manner of unintelligible or embarrassing sobriquets are assigned just by virtue of their popping out of a child's mouth. It gets stuck forever just because everyone oohs and aahs and thinks they're in the presence of genius. Would I allow a toddler to drive my car? No. And I wouldn't let a toddler name me either, thank you.

And I didn't even want to think about how to supply and accessorize a twenty-first-century baby. Way back in the old days, let's say I needed a bottle. I would go to the drugstore and buy one. There were choices, of course—pink, clear, mint green, blue. They came with a cap and a nipple in four-, six-, or twelve-ounce sizes. Simple. Now, however, there are bottle-feeding systems with electronics and encyclopedia-like manuals and their own websites. And clothing is no different. I might have to take a course before I attempted clothes. When I had my babies, there were onesies in three colors: blue for boys, pink for girls, and white for spills. Onesies are still around, but now they are organic cotton or bamboo, fair trade or handmade, Baby Gap or Baby Gucci, all in neutral colors. But not yellow, green, and brown—it's saffron, aloe, and fawn. There are sheets and shoes and pads and beds and strollers that look like Conestoga wagons. There is not a single need left unmarketed to. Nonna Sue even saw a canister of wipes exclusively for wiping fallen pacifiers clean. Don't you just stick it in your mouth, remove the really gritty stuff, and pop it back in Baby's mouth?

What if I had to babysit for the weekend? Where was I going to put our little angel? Not in a drawer, like they did in all the old movies. Was it even okay to get a regular old bassinet without an educational mobile or integrated Baby Einstein motion-detecting video? Did they even make regular cribs anymore?

Like I said, I had a lot to learn. We all did. But we were up for it. Though it was possible that we all needed to take a babymoon first. Oh, you don't know what a babymoon is? It's a trip that the parents-to-be take before the baby arrives. You know, like a honeymoon. I actually sat next to a couple on a train going from Florence to Rome who were on a babymoon. I am not lying. These twenty-first-century parents think of everything! I needed a babymoon.

And I definitely needed to register at Macy's.

Why Do Today What I Can Put Off Until Next Year?

The only reason I had sparkly white Christmas lights hanging in my living room was that I had never taken them down after the previous year's Christmas decorating. I had managed to buy a bag of peppermint Hershey's Kisses and miniature candy canes for my English class's final exam, but my students ate most of the treats, so I didn't even have leftovers for my family. And I had not bought one Christmas present.

If you came into my house, you would not see my reindeer candy dish brimming with M&M's, a Santa-covered photo book of all the Christmas card pictures I've received over the years, or the cute little snowmen that I usually stick here and there to be festive.

There was no tree.

There were no stockings, hung with care or otherwise. In fact, the only decorative, Christmassy item in view in my house besides the lights was the handmade advent calendar that I'd managed to get out on December 1. But as of this day, we did not have sixteen ornaments hanging on it. The emails I received announcing "Last-Minute Specials!" or "Free Shipping—Today Only!" got deleted. I didn't want to think about it. I didn't want to think about Christmas at all.

A clinician stumbling upon this scene might have ordered me up some Cymbalta, but I wasn't depressed. Far from it. I was just too busy looking at my new grandson, Luca. Ever since Annie, Tony, and the baby had moved into my house after Thanksgiving, I'd done nothing but hold the baby, change the baby, bathe the baby, and hold the baby again (or watch other people hold the baby). That takes a lot of time. And energy—especially for "older" me. All my mommy skills had come back in an interesting way: I was more confident in them but slower at them. And my knees hurt more.

No one was getting anything done. Except Tony, that is—and he had to go all the way to Manhattan to do it. I was managing to go to work when I was expected, but then I'd come right back and snatch up Luca from wherever he was and gaze into his face. At six weeks old, he was starting to recognize us, and I was pretty sure he liked me best so far. Obviously I wasn't going to tell anyone that—I think his mommy and daddy might have been put out by this information—but it was clear that I was right. He laughed at all my jokes, and he hadn't peed on me at all. If that wasn't evidence, I didn't know what was.

I'm not the only one who was totally enraptured by this baby. My husband was as swept away as the rest of us. He kept threatening to take him back to Italy—just the two of them. And that shrieking noise you hear is Nonna Sue going out of her mind missing him up in Buffalo. A baby changes everything. Well, duh—we all knew that, didn't we? But I didn't know how much he would change *me*. Christmas, the next several holidays, and probably dusting and laundry would just have to wait. Unless it had to do with the baby, I didn't have time. For the time being, the only thing I was celebrating was Luca.

Holidays

New Year's
Adjustments

The New Year's resolution. Who thought up this idea: this national, subversive trend supposedly designed to empower people to change their lives for the better but that ultimately sabotages all behavior aimed at self-reflection? Probably Hallmark.

The theory is plausible: examine your life and make note of where some change is due. At the first breath of the New Year, the launch of twelve months of possibility, the threshold of potential, vow to all humankind (or any of your close, personal friends who happen to be around) that you will make that change to the best of your ability. You will lose ten pounds, you most definitely will quit smoking, and you will finally put away some money for a rainy day (or a sunny day, say, in Jamaica). This will happen—as God is your witness, let no man put asunder.

Then you order another plate of nachos, light up a cigarette, and buy another round of champagne cocktails for yourself and your friends to celebrate the new you.

Some resolutions may have a longer life than the few seconds after they are uttered. I'm sure there are people out there who take them seriously. All that introspection and taking stock must be good for the soul (or something). People take more time noticing what they aren't doing in their lives, what they haven't accomplished, or who they haven't been nice to today than they did in the past. I don't imagine that the pioneers gathering at the town well on New Year's Eve two hundred years ago were figuring out which piece of their emotional baggage to work on. Today, however, we are encouraged by shrinks, friends, therapists, books, magazine articles, and television infomercials to excavate our psyches. If you find something amiss in your life and it needs improvement, I am willing to bet a study has already been done on it and there's a book and series of workshops out there that will help you fix it. To be honest, I admire such self-repair; I just don't want you to invite me to the party. We all know how much fun it is to hang out with people who spend a lot of time thinking about themselves and then hashing it out with you.

I'm sure I will get in trouble with some of you for being insensitive to those among us who are reflective. Socrates suggested that an unexamined life is not worth living. Maybe so—but an over-examined life is boring. Whatever happened to the natural process of figuring out what needs to be changed? Like listening—not only to yourself, but also to the people around you. Picking up clues from our environment about how to behave is pretty much how people did it before we were all urged to look inside. My opinion? The pendulum has swung a little wide, and in doing so, it has closed many of us off from one another. Eventually, though, it will come back to the middle and we will all live happily ever after in an effectively communicative society that balances self-introspection with symbiosis. Just like algae on lichen—that's how I like to live.

As for New Year's resolutions, I'll give them a shot. Doing what everybody else is doing can't be all bad—in moderation. But, just to be different (something I constantly do, something that I should perhaps consider changing), I will modify the process just a little to give myself a fighting chance. Instead of New Year's resolutions, I will make New Year's adjustments.

Here goes:

I will keep at that ten pounds. (Fine. Twenty.) But in my defense, I did join a gym, and those pounds haven't gone anywhere yet, except on vacation for a little while in the summer. They came right back right between Halloween and Thanksgiving.

I will try to be more patient with my husband . . . as long as *his* resolution is to keep his paintbrushes out of the kitchen sink.

I'll save some money. I'll save. I'll save twenty dollars between January 1st and December 31st, just to prove I can do it.

I think three is enough.

Happy New Year. Wish me luck.

Anniversary

The sky in Avalon at six thirty in the morning was an unbeliev-able shade of pink highlighted by swirly golden clouds. It was my third day at the Jersey shore in a home about twenty yards from the Atlantic Ocean. I sat up in bed, inspired, and thought to myself, *Maybe I'll go out for a run.* And then I remembered: I don't run. I rolled over and went back to sleep.

At about nine, I got up and took the mystery I was in the middle of upstairs to the deck overlooking the beach, to sit with a cup of coffee and read for a while. It was another great morning in what I anticipated would be a great week. I was in New Jersey to celebrate my parents' fiftieth wedding anniversary. My brother, sister, and I had spent the last eleven months trying to organize this event so it would be special and memorable. This was no small feat for the organizationally impaired (read: my brother, my sister, and me). But we gathered tons of food, special activities, and memorabilia, and it was all contained within this lovely beach home, a gift in itself, since the house belonged to a friend who was letting us stay there for free. How lucky were we?

Well, extremely lucky. A fiftieth wedding anniversary is a mile-stone that not too many people will reach in their lives. And the odds against it are greater and greater all the time. I won't celebrate a fiftieth wedding anniversary. And for those who might reach it, it is just as likely one or the other spouse will pass away before it happens. I am not trying to be cynical about fiftieth wedding anniversaries; on the contrary, I'm trying to point out how very special a fiftieth wedding anniversary is, and to reiterate just how lucky we all were to be able to have such an event to share with all concerned parties.

Anniversary is a weighty phenomenon. Our first day in Avalon was September eleventh, but I couldn't bring myself to watch any of the televised, political, schmaltzy, manipulative special events. I am not cynical about 9/11, either. It's just that I am of the school, or perhaps just the classroom, of thought that believes September eleventh should be a national day of remembrance. Weddings shouldn't be planned that day just because the banquet hall is available; soccer games shouldn't be scheduled; instead, we, as a nation, should just sit back, remember, and honor, with reflection and mindfulness, a terrible day when everything we believed about safety, security, and the American way changed. It was a paradigm shift, as far as I am concerned. Not a reason to go to war, and not a reason to limit civil liberties, but rather an event that shook most of us to our very core and changed the way we look at our lives and behave toward our loved ones.

Maybe part of the reason I feel this way is that another anniversary occurs around this time of year: my own wedding anniversary. We were married in 2001, not coincidentally a little over a month after the paradigm shift. We had been planning to get married for at least three years at that point but hadn't quite gotten around to it. (Remember the organizationally challenged folk I mentioned? Angelo is one of them, too.) We were living together, the kids seemed okay with it all, and we'd been going with the "why fix it if it ain't broke?" approach. Then the world changed. And we got married.

Katrina is another anniversary that brings layers of necessary reflection and thought to us as a nation and, to some, as individuals. It was Katrina that moved me to finally write about Sue, my college roommate who was murdered in New Orleans—an event that happened in early 1980. I guess it just takes me longer than others to process some events. But it was New Orleans in the news that brought back to my emotional surface feelings that should have been resolved, or at least buried, by now. And it was that experience that motivated me to commit to my writing and start my blog.

The "anniversary phenomenon" in medicine and psychology is often studied for its impact on people. Patients who suffer specific physical or emotional symptoms at certain times of the year are usually found to have experienced a traumatic event at that time years earlier. I experienced this myself after my appendectomy, which was an enormously traumatic event, both emotionally and physically. (Who gets appendicitis at age forty-two? Me.) It happened on Mother's Day, too, which added to the total hilarity of the event. Because I am the camp counselor of my family, no one was prepared to "care" for me when I came home from the hospital, so I tried to keep up my daily responsibilities to the best of my ability—which was inadequate, and which hindered my recovery. Suffice it to say, it was a pretty unpleasant experience, and every May since, I've gotten a little anxious the week leading up to Mother's Day. Even knowing why doesn't really prevent it, although over the years the anxiety has gotten less intense. Sort of.

Memories, thoughts, feelings, grief, sadness, frustration, anger, physical symptoms, all can be triggered by an anniversary, which, honestly, makes the phrase "happy anniversary" a little presumptuous. Hopefully, most are. Birthdays, first dates, weddings, graduations . . . these are all happy occasions and should be celebrated monthly, yearly, or daily. But anniversary remembers all events, happy or otherwise, and the weight of the term—the depth of it— should be honored for all its power.

Auld Lang Syne*

When the holidays hijack my writing time, I try to make up for it by opening up old files on my computer to see if I can finish previously started essays. It's a shortcut to getting some work done and feeling less guilty. In one instance, I opened a file called "The Wisdom of Men" to see if I could finish that one. Turns out, it needed a little more than finishing up: it was blank. (That's funny, though, isn't it? A document called "The Wisdom of Men" was entirely blank.) At these times, when I am in between topics for essays, one file I consistently avoid is the one called "Family."

Ever since I created the file, I've avoided working on it. It's kind of like having reverse writer's block. I know what I want to write about; I just don't know how to go about writing it. I'm the boy with his finger in the dyke. My words, like the sea, are behind the wall, pressuring me to just let go and let them pour forth. All I have to do is move my finger(s) and let them come, but I keep feeling like I need to stem the flow.

The problem is, once I let this come forward, I may not have any control whatsoever over its eventual path. And writing about family is touchy. Others may not see things the way I do, might not agree that I have the right to discuss private matters in eight hundred words or fewer with strangers. That's the way it is with families, right? Oh well, let's see what happens.

So . . . families. God bless that mess, huh? Over the last few months, I've experienced more than the usual amount of required, intense family interactions—both positive and negative. Sweet and sad. Loving and painful. Neurotic and psychotic. And to think I used to want a bigger family. Before I was divorced, I thought I'd have two or three more kids. When I met my present husband, I thought we'd have at least one together. But it wasn't to be. I've got my three: two biological and one technological. And it's actually more than enough to handle. Managing the family of birth takes all the time you've got on this sweet earth already, but then you go ahead and start adding those others—those in-laws and out-laws and firsts and seconds and distants and formers and by-marriages—and where's a scorecard when you need one? And how about culture splicing? That's always fun. My family is mostly a bunch of pretty mild, blue-eyed, and blond Swedes. Some of us, and not just me, have some Italian thrown into the mix (and it's actually a fairly workable mix, since eating is high on the priority list of most family get-togethers). We've got a little Irish as well, and my kids bring in some German from their dad's side of the family. So, despite the Allies/Axis thing, most of our time together is quite fun. *Most* of it.

Apart from the ethnicity-and-culture thing, there are ancient family dynamics involved. My husband and I are both the oldest child in our family of birth, so naturally both of us know everything. (It's a picnic every day.) We both have two younger siblings, and they each have spouses and kids. His parents passed away, so he occasionally borrows mine for birthdays and holidays. They like him well enough, so it works all the way around.

I guess when the going gets rough are the times when all the different dynamics, cultures, and hierarchies collide. For instance, when we celebrated my parents' fiftieth wedding anniversary, it was remarkable that we didn't kill each other during the whole week we were together, especially as my brother had a video camera pointed in my parents' faces for most of the trip in order to document the event. But in spite of that, it went exceedingly well, considering that my family hadn't been alone together in more than twenty years.

A couple of months after the anniversary trip, in December, we buried a beloved uncle, and although the experience was deeply sad and emotional, it brought us face-to-face with the ways in which we all express our grief. It also gave us an uncomfortable peek into the not-so-distant future, when we will each deal with death on much closer terms. The months in between brought situations when communications were misinterpreted and apologies went unaccepted. Painful, but—through the lens of a reality that accepts dynamics, culture, and individuality as just part of the mix—acceptable. As for the neuroses, well, there's always a dose of neuroses to add a little spice.

It seems that at this time of year, people always talk about their families with a depth of emotion I don't notice the rest of the year. Families are a huge responsibility, in good times and bad, but I guess I'd rather have one than not. Plus, the video from the anniversary turned out pretty well. And, as if we were members of the Academy, we all got a copy.

Would you borrow a pair of underwear from anyone but your sister? Does anyone but your brother drive your car? Is anyone getting the recipe to Nonna's cookies but Nonna's daughter or granddaughter (or possibly Nonna's grandson's girlfriend's mother, who's not Italian but is a darn good Swedish cookie baker)? All in all, from who else but a family member would you want a kidney? Or a pint of blood? They are who we are, they are where we come from. God bless us, every one.

Auld lang syne may be translated literally as "old long since" or, more idiomatically, "long ago" or "days gone by."

Happy Thanks Giving

I ran into a coworker the other day—I'll call her Andie—as I was coming down the stairs to the copy room. Two years ago, during Thanksgiving break, she suddenly lost her husband. In the year that followed, people were understanding—murmuring condolences and sympathy when they saw her—but after a time, things went back to normal.

Although I don't know Andie outside of work, when the holiday came around again, I thought about how this anniversary—one that comes during a time when all the talk and greetings are about being thankful—must be a particularly difficult one. It's not as if I write down dates like this, or that I always remember them (for others or even for myself—I always confuse the date of my own wedding anniversary), but when I do remember, I feel compelled to say something. So when I ran into Andie on the stairs, I reached over, patted her on the arm, and said, "How are you doing today?"—and she knew exactly what I was talking about.

As we headed into the copy room together, she told me she was doing much better this year than last. She still honored the memory of her husband and all the things they shared, but she was in a whole different place now. Not that it was easy. She said she spent the first year emotionally holed up, but during the second year she began to see the ways in which what had happened to her—an experience her previously sheltered life had left her unprepared for—could lead her to be a better person. In fact, she now had a whole list of things that she wanted to do, a list that grew longer and longer as she worked through the loss that had so devastatingly changed her life.

One of the things Andie decided needed some adjustment was how to regard the passage of time. For her, the idea that other people should get to decide how much time she needed to "get over" something didn't make sense. Who had the right to decide for her how long it should take for her to "get over" the death of her husband? What if it took her only one year? What if it took five? How is it anyone's business but that of the one who is dealing with such a loss?

Andie's words rang true to me. People get uncomfortable when you don't meet their time requirements for recovering from a loss. Discomfort sets in, and they don't want to talk about something that happened so long ago. And then the grief-stricken start to be avoided, as if they've disappointed everyone else's expectations. Andie said she felt like people were afraid to talk to her after her husband's death because they thought something might happen to them, as if her sadness were contagious, but she still wanted to be able to talk about it because it was so important to her and had changed her whole life. Nothing wrong there.

The other thing about time, Andie said, is that there's none to waste. In addition to the many things she remembered doing with her husband, there were many things that she regretted not having done. Why? Because there was always Saturday. Or next summer. Or when we have enough money or can take the time off from work. Better to just do it now and enjoy the time you have, she said—because while suddenly losing your husband is not contagious, it does happen, and it can happen to anybody at any time. The days, weeks, and years will pass no matter what. Might as well spend them doing something you want to do.

Another item on Andie's to-do list was to say something. To others. Out loud. Every day. Clearly this isn't something I need to add to my own list, since, as I explained to Andie, I am a blurter. My foot goes in and out of my mouth on a pretty regular basis; I can usually be counted on to say the most inappropriate thing at the most inopportune time. The lesson I took away from this item on her list, though, was to learn to become more comfortable with this particular tendency of mine. In a way, it's the very thing that allowed me to connect with Andie that day—as uncomfortable as it can be to speak to someone about her pain or loss, I couldn't help but say something to her.

As Andie and I left the copy room, and she went her way and I went mine, all I could think about was how incredible it is that after having been put through the fire, she was coming out of it with a smile on her face and a bright green scarf around her shoulders—and a willingness to share this most private journey of hers with others. If that's not a happy thanks giving, I don't know what is.

And So This
Is Christmas

I don't recall ever having wished I had more at Christmas, although family lore puts me squarely in the role of present-counter year after year. Frankly, I attribute my attentiveness to a developing attitude of social justice and fairness, rather than a strong urge to tick off whether or not Susie got a Chatty Cathy under the tree or Richard got more candy in his stocking. (They did.)

As the eldest and nosiest child, I was the first one to discover the neat pile of presents in "Santa" wrap hiding in my dad's old college trunk behind the washing machine, under the boxes of old dishes, in the basement. For a few years after that, I was keenly aware of where all the presents came from: not from a huge canvas sack shoved down the chimney during a split-second visit on Christmas Eve, but from Thornbury's Toys in St. Matthew's. I remember feeling a kind of importance, as if I had just been given membership to a special, grown-up club now that I Knew. The number of presents and stocking stuffers didn't really matter—I just needed to make sure that my little brother and sister were distracted enough on Christmas morning that they wouldn't accidentally learn The Truth. Those of us who Knew were fine with what few presents we received, because we were the ones charged with perpetuating the all-important myth of Santa. And in our family, he was one generous guy.

Years went by, and my memory still held Christmas as a time of abundance. Even when I was in college, I got to fly home to Louisville from Austin, use the car to drive around and see my friends, and eat tons of my dad's homemade Spritz cookies—and I still had a stocking to dump out on the couch and presents under the tree to open. Of course, Susie still got more stuff than I did, even though by this time she also knew. (But, really, what does that matter now? I barely even remember that part.)

My hindsight sees holiday abundance even during my poor, single-mom years. Yes, once or twice I had to "shop" at the charity event our church participated in for those who were without during the holiday season—but since I was the church secretary, I was allowed to pre-shop on the sly, thereby maintaining some pride and secrecy. If my kids compared their haul with those of their more affluent friends and felt under-gifted, they didn't let on to me.

When the big night came, we always hosted a Christmas Eve open house in between the children's pageant at five and the midnight service at eleven, and our table brimmed with hand-decorated cookies, Swedish meatballs, homemade limpa rye bread, and a Crock-Pot full of warm mulled cider. There were candles in our windows and a tree in the family room, the stockings were hung with care—on the windowsill, since we didn't have a mantel upon which to place them—and in the morning they would be full of as many little Pez dispensers, hair scrunchies, cassette tapes, and trading cards as I could afford.

These were the years when the "big" presents were the handpainted sweatshirts I made for both Annie and Christopher. I would commemorate some significant event and create a unique design in fabric paint, working in secret at night when the kids were in bed, then wrap them lovingly and place them under the tree. I know they looked forward to them each year and appreciated the work and love I put into them. (I know this because I haven't seen any of those sweatshirts since—owing, I am certain, to the fact that my children put them away somewhere safe so they can keep them forever, possibly even hand them down to their own children on some future Christmas morning.) It might seem that on these Christmases we didn't have a lot . . . but to me, it felt like we had plenty.

These days, that feeling of abundance continues to be a part of my Christmas anticipation. Financially, I am better off now than when I was a single parent, but I haven't won the lottery or become the CEO of a financial services company, so I still budget my Christmas giving. Sure, I wish I could take everyone to the islands for Christmas, buy a new car with the obligatory enormous red bow on top, or provide new laptops or video cameras wrapped under the tree. But I can't—and I wonder, if I had ever been able to do that, would it have changed the way I see Christmas? Would I have always been focused on the next bigger, better, more expensive thing I could get? I imagine that having a bigger bank account would change one of my time-honored traditions: instead of choosing the free Super Saver shipping and having to print out little pictures of the gifts I've purchased, I could pay a little more so the presents I order on December 17 might actually arrive in time for me to put them under the tree.

I also wonder if I would ever think about the *other* way of giving if I had tons of money. When I was really struggling, the only way I could give to others was with my time. And I'll be honest: I didn't really give all that much of it. I would sign up with my kids to do a shift at the soup kitchen, or we would buy a pair of gloves for the mitten tree at school, but I wasn't in a position to really make a dent in the need so many people endure—not just during the holidays, but year-round. When I got to the place in my life where I had a little extra money in my pocket, I felt like I should do more, so one year I gave geese and ducks and chickens as presents through Heifer International. One year, I gave through Kiva. It still wasn't much, but it was a little more than I was able to do before—and hopefully not as much as I will be able to do in the years to come.

I've always liked it when there's a winter storm or bad weather of some sort on December 23 or 24. It puts paid to the holiday preparations. You'd better be done, or you'll have to risk life and limb for a Lindt chocolate Santa or that underappreciated red scarf you buy during your final mad dash to the store on Christmas Eve.

Last-minute anxiety disappears as soon as you wake up on Christmas morning, because what you've got is what you've got. In our family we're lucky: we have a lot to give and a lot to receive, and on Christmas morning we are happy, warm, slightly tipsy from mimosas, and dangerously close to comatose from too many chocolates. For all the things I could be in therapy about, dealing with disappointing Christmases isn't one of them. Abundance doesn't come wrapped—it comes from within.

All Grown Up

A Real Grown-Up

When I was twelve years old, I got my hair cut. I don't remember why; maybe it was for a party or a school dance or the dreaded yearly school pictures. I can only guess that it was an attempt at looking older than I was. I have always been . . . hmm, how shall I put this? My grandma always called me "pleasingly plump." I probably thought I would seem taller, or thinner, or a little more like Hayley Mills. However, rather than looking more sophisticated with the new 'do, I ended up looking like a thick lump of a child in a neighborhood full of skinny little girls with flopping pigtails who were always running around on tan, thin legs dressed in short cutoff shorts. I still have a picture in my head of what it looked like: my round little face, my once-long hair stopping abruptly above my shoulders. I began to hate my haircut. I needed something on my body to be long and thin, and before my haircut, that thing had been my hair. When you are pleasingly plump, you don't want much else on your body to be short and chunky. So I started letting it grow.

On it grew, through high school and college and into adulthood, gracing my short, chunky body with long—and then longer—blond hair. Well, mostly blond. And sometimes with bangs. (Ugh—I never learned the bangs lesson.) My role model was my maternal grandmother, who I think was the world's first divorced single parent. She was an artist in New York City in the early 1940s and '50s. Not the bohemian, absinthe-sipping, hanging-out-with-de Kooning kind, but the paint-family-portraits-on-the-side-while-drawing-for-the-Montgomery Ward-catalog kind. As the world's first divorced single parent to my mother, she was required to be Responsible. So she wound her long, silver-blond hair tightly into a bun and bound it with a black velvet ribbon. As a child I always tried to visualize what it would look like if she ever let it loose. I imagined that, like the Grimms' Goose Girl, she would make the wind chase people away so she could comb it out in all its silvery beauty.

Then, one year, the unthinkable happened: right after she turned sixty-five, she cut it all off. I remember the photograph she took to commemorate the deed. It wasn't the shortness that was so shocking; it had always looked short up in the bun anyway. What was shocking was that she had done it at all. *Wow*, I thought. *Like a grown-up*. It was wonderful news for me, because I knew then that I had at least forty-five years to go before I needed to even think about cutting my hair.

So, what did I do well before the sixty-five-year mark for hair cutting and growing up? I gave in. I gave my hairstylist complete authorization to cut it all off.

"Do you want to cut it to your shoulders?" she asked.

Images of female East German athletes leaped in front of my eyes. "*No!*" I think I screamed a little. "Take advantage of my bravery—cut!" I commanded.

"Do you want to try bangs?" she asked.

I couldn't listen anymore. "Don't ask me any more questions—just do it!" I shrieked. Clearly, in my boldness, I had again forgotten the bangs lesson. I closed my eyes and she turned the chair away from the mirror. She started cutting.

An important codicil here: my body is *not* any less short or chunky now than it was when I was twelve. I didn't suddenly become a supermodel. So what in God's name was I thinking? I suspect it was the growing-up part. I can make my hair look decent when it lies in lengths below my shoulders, but I just can't shake the idea that almost-fifty-year-olds should have a "hairstyle."

Plus, there is the graying thing that's happening. My gray hair is definitely not long or thin. It is obdurate and annoying. It pokes up from my scalp like so many broken bedsprings, and the effect is ridiculous. The final factor, however, was the Internet. I found a website called Makeover-o-Matic. I uploaded a picture and straight away began the makeover. I tried short hair, curly hair, even Beyoncé hair. With the false confidence that these virtual before-and-after shots gave me, I called and made the appointment. And the rest, as they say, is history.

And then my hair was short. Really short. And not the short it was when I left the salon, because we all know they work some scary magic there that allows your hair to look perfectly coiffed only once. No, I have the one-side-goes-this-way-and-the-other-side-goes-that-way kind of short hair now. No number of head-bands, barrettes, or black velvet ribbons will help me. I made my choice, and now I have to live with it. If that isn't growing up, I don't know what is.

Alone Again, Naturally

Remember that song? Gilbert O'Sullivan? "In a little while from now, if I'm not feeling any less sour . . ."

Totally an anthem for the angst-ridden fourteen-year-old of 1972 (which I was). I would sit in my room and pose plaintively in front of the full-length mirror with my best soulful eyes and my hair hanging like a shroud around my face so I could prove, when the photographers came to capture my passion, that I deserved my very own eight-by-ten glossy in *Tiger Beat*. I was all alone—very dramatic.

My mom quoted the lyric to me when she called me and asked, "Are you having a good time?" My husband was away, out West to visit his daughter, and I was managing the best I could without him in the snowy Northeast. Was I having a good time? (Don't read this, honey . . .) Absolutely!

Of course I missed him. We don't have jobs that take us traveling away from each other much, so we're pretty used to spending each and every ever-lovin' minute of our lives together—when we're not at work, of course. But even then, we email each other ten to fifteen times a day. Days, nights, weekends—we're there, together. All the time. Joined at the hip, we are. So when he decided to visit his daughter in Arizona and asked me, "Will you be okay?" I blinked my eyes with feigned helplessness, pretended to think a minute, and responded with a faltering "Oh,

I'm sure I'll be fine. Don't worry about me." Inside, though, I thought: *Whoopee!*

It's not that I wanted to get rid of my husband. Not at all. There was snow in the forecast, and who would shovel if he left? But I'm a big girl now and I figured I could manage. No, I didn't figure I could; I knew I could.

Years ago, when I got a divorce and joined the ranks of single parents, I had my two kids, a newly acquired apartment, and my parents' old car—and that was pretty much it. I was the one who moved out, not him. I didn't get the house, the credit cards, or a big fat alimony check every month. I barely got child support. Talk about your rude awakenings!

The first few months were killer. I drove my kids to their dad's house every Sunday afternoon after church; they would stay with him for a few days, and then they would come and meet me at work after school on Wednesday. I would wear my tan leather jacket to church, and on the ride home, after I dropped the kids off at their dad's, it would catch my tears. I thought of the little stains the tears left on the leather as badges—emblems of my singlehood. And so it went, Sunday after Sunday, tear after tear.

The first few weeks, I'd get home and just sort of wander through the house. Not do anything productive, like dust or laundry—just wander. I didn't know who I was without my kids. I was so lonely. I'd always had someone around to care for or talk to or yell at or bathe or feed. Now I didn't. What was I supposed to do?

The first thing that occurred to me to do was have a glass of wine—or three, or four. The oenophile in me opted for big-bottle wine; five dollars and ninety-nine cents was an inexpensive way to make the days go by really fast. It was also a really good way to acquire furniture and household items, since the catalogs that had followed me when I moved all had very helpful twenty-four-hour operators standing by for my order. At 2:00 AM, turns out, you can get right through! Thank God I was divorced before Amazon. I also went to work and wrote in my journal. (In a throwback to fourteen,

I was once again the lonely heroine stalwartly braving the wrath of the evil prince, knowing that someday he'd be vanquished and I'd live to love again. *Tiger Beat*, where were you when I needed you?)

But one Sunday afternoon, as I sat at my new kitchen café set and sipped coffee from my new blue-and-white crockery mugs, I looked around and I liked where I was. That day, I wasn't lonely anymore; I was just alone. And alone was just fine. Suddenly I knew what to do after I dropped my kids off. I visited with friends, worked in my garden or read, and the days went by just fine without my five ninety-nine wine—and quickly, too. Being alone wasn't much different from being with my kids, really. I still missed them every minute, of course. And I continued to add to my badge collection each week. But at some point I stopped being sad about being alone; in fact, I started liking it, and I liked that I liked it. At the risk of sounding trite, I think it made me a stronger, more independent person. And there is nothing wrong with being a strong, independent person—especially when you are raising children on your own.

But back to my weekend alone. There were several events I could have attended, and I definitely could have made a trip or two to the gym. But I stayed home. I made a list of things I wanted to get done, laid in some wood—it was going to snow, remember?—and found a good, thick book to read. And, yeah, I got a little wine, too. By the time my mom called on Sunday night, I had enjoyed four days to myself and had two more to go. I'd gotten most of my list crossed off, finished my book, and even gone out to the grocery a few times. And I'd shoveled the driveway, too. (Badly, yes—but that's not really the point, is it?) And I liked it. I love being with my husband, kids, family, and friends—but I enjoy my own company just as much. So when my husband is gone and the choice is mine? I choose alone. Naturally.

Reunion

The book *Passages*, by Gail Sheehy, was published in 1976—the year, coincidentally, that I graduated from high school. It covers "the years between 18 and 50 [that] are the center of life, a time of growth and opportunity," and the back cover claims that "until now no guide has existed to help us understand the mysterious process by which we become adults." Although it sounds like I should have picked it right up at the time, "passages," whatever they were, didn't concern me. As far as I knew, passages were the secret hallways in haunted mansions that the heroes find when it's time to save the pretty blond girl chained in the basement of the weird mad scientist who's about to turn her into a sex slave/zombie. Or something.

Turns out, however, that there are a bunch of passages in a given life. Sometimes you notice them while they're happening; other times, it's only upon reflection that you realize you've just been through one. High school is one, but it's one of the ones you don't notice because you're too consumed with what you're going to wear that morning because it's Tuesday and you can't wear your cute blue Indian blouse until Friday so you can wear it with your new white pants to the big party after the basketball game that night. Who can pay attention to developmental passages when there are outfits to put together? I suppose high school requires other energies as well, like taking time to prepare ourselves for adulthood and careers by visiting with guidance counselors to pick colleges. I guess that's what we did. Frankly, I don't remember. Whatever I was going to do after high school—go to an out-of-state university, stay in-state, or go work at the mall—none of it mattered more than the task at hand: making sure I went to the prom and at least one party after graduation.

But passages came, whether I was prepared or not. I went to an out-of-state school. I stayed in touch with some of my high school friends for a while. I spent my twenties falling in love, getting married, having babies, and moving several times, crisscrossing the South. My thirties were occupied with holding a marriage together and then watching it—painfully—fall apart while trying to keep my kids reasonably sane (though I didn't always quite manage the same for myself). I began my forties as a single parent to two pretty amazing kids who had survived a divorce. Then, since those passages went so well, I decided to go back to school for a master's degree. It was one of those times when a guidance counselor could have been helpful, but I didn't seek one out that time, either. And, to complete the hat trick, I got married to a wonderful man who added, among other things, a lovely stepdaughter to my family. Passages galore.

Then it was time for my high school's thirtieth reunion. The call went out months before the event, and at the time, although I told the one remaining friend with whom I've kept in touch that I would come, I wasn't really sure I would. Most memories I have of that time in my life are sketchy, but there are certain moments that I recall with a grimace. I believe the Greek translation for the name Cindy is "awkward." How in the world could I reconcile who I was then with the person I am now? Not only that, but attend several events with loads of former classmates? I could feel myself starting to sweat. . . .

And then I realized—it wasn't like I was going *back* to high school. I traversed that passage, thorny though it was. I did it, maybe not successfully, by some measures, but it's done nevertheless. And I've weathered subsequent passages as well—some with difficulty and some pretty well, again depending on whose account you believe. High school, college, marriage, parenthood, life . . . I haven't come this far, and gotten this old, just to go back to where I began. This reunion was a substantial milestone that I was happy to celebrate. I felt lucky to be in a place where I could look forward to attending an event that marked my having survived over a certain number of years, with others who had done the same. And whose memories were, hopefully, just as hazy as mine.

Still, I obsessed over the reunion for the last month or so before it happened. It was a reunion; I had trepidations about it. But when haven't I wrestled with trepidations about hanging out with these people? Trepidation was my signature emotion in high school, and, combined with an out-of-this-world imagination, it made for a bizarre way to pass through those years. I would drift in and out of different conversations in high school, included in some, not in others, and over the course of the day I would hear about parties or dates or basketball games. Sometimes they'd say, "Hey, Cindy, are you going?" and I'd end up waiting at home that night as if I were going to get picked up any minute (though I wasn't really sure I wanted to be)—but the call never came. By the end of the night, I'd usually end up watching TV with my brother and sister. I guess at the time I felt hurt or slighted or whatever, but I don't think I ever felt it was done *to* me. I just chalked it up to not being pretty or popular enough, or not possessing whatever the necessary magic ingredients for inclusion were.

Surprisingly, during my fifty-five hours in Louisville, I discovered that I was not the only one who felt that way. The first event was on Friday night, a delightful boat cruise on the Ohio River. But I actually didn't get on the boat. It felt like it was too much, too soon, for me. Instead, my friend Diane and I stayed onshore, getting some food in our stomachs in anticipation of the onslaught of alcohol that was sure to follow. As we sat at our table on the deck of Captain's Quarters in the near-perfect twilight, familiar faces started showing up in the crowd. The years had been much kinder to the girls than to the boys (sorry, boys, no offense), and I recognized all of them. As we talked, the same nervous statement was repeated over and over: "I didn't think anyone would even recognize me/talk to me." The boat came back and the crowd grew. More familiar faces, this time with identification, as the boat people were required to wear name tags. (Hɪ! My name is . . . *Really? That's you?*) So many people, so many memories. In a word: overwhelming. And there were still two more events the next day. I wasn't sure I would make it. But later that night, as I sank into my bed at the hotel, the main thought among the million contradictory ones swirling in my head was *So far, so good.*

The next day included a class of '76 memorial race at Churchill Downs and a dinner dance in the evening. I skipped the afternoon races at the Downs to hang out in downtown Louisville and tour the old neighborhoods with Diane. But we went to dinner on Saturday night, and everyone looked beautiful, and we were all best friends. (Yes, even the boys looked great—maybe not exactly the same, but in many cases better.)

Back in high school, we were all in our own little worlds, thinking no one liked us or that they thought we weren't good enough for them, or whatever. We spent four years within that social framework. It is collectively a formative, and individually an emotionally significant, time for each of us, yet we all experienced it in unique ways. At dinner that night, however—now that we were all this old and this far away from our high school careers—the playing field was finally level. We either couldn't remember or didn't care to remember all the minutiae of our individual experiences—and what we *could* remember was transmuted to a greater shared experience. It was, in a word, amazing. The social democrat in me wonders what we could achieve together if we wanted to impact change in our society . . . but maybe that's for the next reunion.

All in all, I was glad I attended. I even got to excavate and dispose of a teeny-tiny, leftover piece of emotional baggage I had carried around for thirty years. (Yes, of course it involved a boy—when doesn't it?) And then, with maturity and wisdom, I left the party. I didn't let my nerves talk me into a third glass of wine, which would have invited my inner smart-ass to appear, and I got to talk to most of the people I wanted to (and even a couple I didn't expect to).

Then, in the elevator on the way up to my room, one of my new best friends told me that a group was meeting in the lobby bar to go out and keep the party going downtown. I promised I'd meet them down there in a few, and as I walked to my room I almost wrenched my shoulder patting myself on the back for accepting the invitation, thrilled with my newfound confidence. I changed my shoes and went back down in the elevator, smiling self-assuredly and thinking to myself how fitting it was that this weekend would end in this way—me, out with the group I'd never really felt a part of in high school but was now being invited to join because time and experience had leveled the playing field. I guessed I could get that other glass of wine now. Except that when I went into the lobby bar where we were all supposed to meet, they weren't there.

I went back to my room, got some ice for my shoulder, poured that other glass of wine, kicked my shoes off, sat back, and smiled. Actually, *this* was the truly fitting way to end the night: I was happily alone in my comfortable hotel room with an amazingly soft bed that I had all to myself. I put up my feet up and I listened to a little music, drank a little wine, munched on some cheese and crackers, and reflected. Yes, it was a good weekend indeed.

In the end, there were promises to keep in touch and exchanges of emails and addresses. And hugging—lots and lots of hugging. As I said my good-byes, there were so many emotions competing for attention in my heart and thoughts that it was hard to guess what the future would hold. But there was one thing I did know: I had attended my high school reunion, and I'd had a good time. My old insecurities had come along for the ride, but they'd left at some point and I hadn't even noticed. The verdict? I wouldn't go back to high school for anything—but I'll attend a reunion anytime.

Well, Shut My Mouth!

There is an old fable I love to recall, a story of a frog and a scorpion. I don't remember where or under what circumstances I first heard it, but here goes:

It seems the frog arrived at the riverbank about the same time as the scorpion. The frog nervously regarded the scorpion as he started to go into the river to cross to the other side. But before he could get into the water, the scorpion spoke.

"Wait!" he said. "Would you take me across the river on your back, please?"

The frog looked back at the scorpion and said, "Are you crazy? You'll sting me!"

"No," the scorpion said, "I promise I won't. I have to get over to the other side for some really important business. Please take me—I don't have any other way to get across."

"Don't play me," the frog said. "I know better. We'll get halfway across and you'll sting me."

"Why would I do that?" the scorpion asked. "Then I wouldn't get across either!"

It went back and forth for a while, but in the end, the frog saw the sense in what the scorpion was saying. If he got stung, neither of them would get over to the other side of the river. He agreed to take him.

So they set off. The scorpion climbed upon the frog's back, and the frog slid easily into the water. Halfway across the river, the scorpion reared his tail and plunged the stinger into the frog's neck.

"Why did you do that?" the frog cried out. "Now we'll both drown!"

"I can't help it," the scorpion replied. "I'm a scorpion."

It's the same story when you're a smart-ass. I'd like to promise I won't say something sarcastic, or snide, or wry—but when push comes to shove, or frog, I can't shut my mouth to save my life. To prove this, I am going to tell you a story. The fact that I am even considering putting it down in print is a testament to my inability to shut up, but I feel confident I can mask the really incriminating stuff.

There was once someone to whom I should never have spoken—ever. A former boss. It's not that I ever did anything terrible to her; we just had an unfortunate chemistry. We were never on the same page. I suppose she just didn't happen to appreciate my particular brand of humor . . . or my general existence. And a thinking person in my position would have known to keep her berth wide and her mouth shut. But, God help me, I just couldn't. For some reason, my boss was my dream straight man (well, woman, really). She set 'em up; I knocked 'em out of the park. And not just occasionally—all the time. All the damn time. At any given work function, I'd be minding my own business until I heard her utter a completely innocent remark, at which point I would respond with some smart-ass comment—brilliant, obviously, but totally unappreciated.

One time, there were witnesses. This is what happened: One late spring day, the administration decided to invite all the employees outside for an ice-cream social. It was in the middle of the workday, so obviously we were all in our work clothes—some of us dressy, some of us more casual. As luck would have it, I was behind my boss in line when she scooped up a big ol' bowl of ice cream, drizzled some chocolate sauce over it, covered the whole concoction with whipped cream, and exclaimed, "I feel just like a little girl again!" I looked over at her spiked black heels, skintight black skirt, and animal-print off-the-shoulder blouse and said, "In that outfit?" The coworkers behind me in line immediately scattered, shaking their heads in disbelief. They didn't even hang around long enough to get their dessert. I quickly filled my own bowl with ice cream (why waste an opportunity like that?) and ran after them, pleading, "Why? Why do I do that?" They didn't know and retreated back into the building. So, as I sat alone and savored my chocolate and vanilla sundae with whipped cream and a maraschino cherry on that sunny spring day, I thought about it, and what I came up with was this: I'm a scorpion. I just can't help it.

I would like to change, but I can't. I'm a smart-ass, and I come from a long line of smart-asses; to change would be untrue to my people. Frankly, this realization reassures me. I admit there are many times when I take pleasure—some might call it a perverse pleasure—in delivering, in ten words or fewer, a perfect, incisive remark that shines a spotlight on someone's irrational social behavior or professional imperfection. I'm not going to change who I am. So the change must come in how I handle the aftermath. Once the words have escaped my mouth, I must develop a strategy—or several—for damage control. For instance, I could look around quickly and exclaim, "Who said that?" Lame, I know, but it's a possibility. Or I could just make sure my mouth is constantly full with either hors d'oeuvres or drink at social functions, thereby masking any utterances that spew forth. I might need to apologize for spitting Chex Mix on someone's shirt, but that's minor compared with the alternative, like, say, getting fired. Maybe I could try keeping my distance from those people who have no appreciation for the mental aptitude it takes to come up with such delightful verbal volleys. Yeah, maybe—but it would take some practice.

It all comes down to taking responsibility. It always does. I try to learn my lessons, I really do. But maybe I'm not paying attention to the real lesson. It wouldn't be the first time. All these years, I've thought I had to change who I was in order to be accepted and move forward in this life. What I've discovered is that I can be who

I am; I just have to accept that others get to be who *they* are, too. And we all don't have to get along; we don't have to be each other's best friend. (At least I don't, because I can't. Believe me, I've tried.) Either people will appreciate who you are or they won't, but that doesn't mean you both don't get an even shot at living this life in the best way you can. Whether you are a frog or a scorpion.

A Very White Girl

In my work with multicultural education and cultural competency, I often stop and attempt to take a reading of where I stand in it all—but I can never actually tell my place in the melting pot (although the term "melting pot" itself is passé, if not downright culturally incompetent, as it suggests we all melt together as one). On official forms and documentation, I am listed as Caucasian, but I don't know what that means. I could have looked it up before I wrote this so as not to appear ignorant of a term I've chosen as representative of me all these years, of course, but then it would seem as though I've known all this time what I was doing each time I checked off that little box. And I didn't.

I do know that I'm white. And if I hadn't known it already, it was confirmed for me recently by one of my doctors. (By the way, as one ages, one apparently begins to amass doctors for varied and specific malfunctions of the body and its systems. Now I have a regular MD, an OB-GYN—although I don't need the OB part anymore—a dentist, an ophthalmologist, and an endocrinologist.) It was my Hispanic endocrinologist who cleared up any misconceptions I might have about my race, or at least my skin color. She was examining a mole on my shoulder blade, and as she tugged down my shirt to give her black-eyed, brown-skinned intern a better look, she expressed her concern at the specimen because "this is a very white girl." The words didn't offend so much as make me suddenly feel like I was glowing—like I was a bright white mushroom on a dark, verdant forest floor.

Then came an opportunity to attend the annual National Association for Multicultural Education (NAME) conference, held that year in Phoenix, Arizona. If I didn't feel bright white before, I sure did that week. I held few expectations of what the experience might be like before I went; my professional involvement in this work was limited. My personal experience with diversity goes a little deeper. Growing up in Louisville, Kentucky, gave me some exposure to race issues—especially when forced busing came along in my senior year of high school. As a senior, I got on the bus each morning and rode it to the school I had gone to for the last five years. My younger sister, however, got on a bus and rode it downtown to Central High School, where she experienced, among other things, having grape soda dumped on her long blond hair while she was in a stall in the girls' bathroom. I drove by the spray-painted bed sheets staked on suburban lawns fervently advocating "No more forced *bussing*," but I didn't live with them in my yard, or even in my neighborhood.

It was only after I went to Texas for college that I experienced being a minority for the first time. The school I attended ran a migrant program called CAMP, College Assistance for Migrants Program, and in some of my classes, the white students were the smaller percentage. All I had to do was go back to my dorm to become one of the majority again, but I was at the very least aware of the disparity. I have always been aware of race, color, and culture, in fact; I've just never known the right way to talk about it. Is the term Hispanic or Latino/a? Is it Black or African American? Indian? Asian? Euro? God help me, I don't want to offend anyone.

I traveled to Arizona for the NAME conference with my bright white light shining before me, clearing the path of any discomfort I might feel, all the while commending myself for being a nonjudgmental, nonbiased, nonracist attendee. Never have I been more aware of the lightness of my skin, the insignificance of my culture, as I was there. Yet it wasn't until one of the workshops on the last day that I felt the depth of my unrest. I had been to "White Privilege 101," I had applauded appreciatively for the young Native American girls and boys who had performed at our opening night, I had joined hands with the women at the morning yoga sessions. I was feeling good. Then I walked into the session called "I'm Not the Indian You Thought I Was." I actually had questions on the topic, so I figured this was as good a place as any to clear them up.

The workshops were only an hour and fifteen minutes long, a short interval to absorb the wisdom of each presenter. This particular presenter kept us engaged and working from the moment we walked in. At one point, a man spoke about his experience in teaching young students, all the while acknowledging his whiteness. The presenter said, "Well at least you're not blond." Ten minutes later, she turned to me and asked me how I felt about her statement. I replied that I was surprised that she had said it but didn't feel compelled to address it. She went on to respond to the question I had brought up earlier—"Is 'Indian summer' a derogatory term?"—and to explain that any discrimination, even discrimination against white blonds, was wrong, and that it was the responsibility of all to stop it. I agreed.

Later, I thought about the session and the presenter's statement. I was in yet another panel discussion, but I withdrew into my own little world for a few minutes to try and understand the new and unfamiliar feeling spreading through me. As I reflected on that last session, I realized how I'd felt when she'd made her statement: I'd felt deserving. I felt deserving of ridicule, bias, laughter, and discrimination. Why? Well, that's a whole other therapy session, but part of it was my credentials. I was at a conference populated by PhDs and EdDs and published authors and doctoral candidates. What could I bring to the table as a measly MEd? On top of that, I think I carry a component of white guilt with me. Although I work in education, I am actively conscious of my own biases and discriminatory feelings. I think I speak up when I see bias, and I teach cultural competency to high school students. Yet I am still a part of a race, a culture, with a long history of subjugating other races and cultures just because they were "other."

This was a tough conference to attend, but at the same time it was a transformative event in my life. Although I experienced the feeling of deserving discrimination there, the realizations that came out of that experience contributed an important element to my evolving self. I know that I'm lucky that generations of my family were not subjected to nationally endorsed discrimination, and even this tiny bit of empathy and understanding can inform my work.

It is a rocky path to travel. But it's a path I was grateful to start down, and it's one that I will probably continue along. I think I'm cut out for it. I am comfortable with being uncomfortable. I'd better be—I get myself into enough uncomfortable situations. There were people from all over the country at that conference, all of them coming together for education and connections, sharing diversity and individuality. Why would we want to homogenize? No wonder we don't want to be a "melting pot" anymore. We'd end up being a great big country of light gray.

Onward Through the Fog

In 2007, I did something startlingly different from my typical behavior: I bought a CD. And not because I am in the habit of downloading music from the Internet—that would be illegal. No, I don't buy CDs because I am just not that into music. I do have my favorites, which I listen to when I'm working . . . when I remember to put them on my iPod. Usually, I will hear something someone else is playing and I'll think to myself, *Oh, this is a good album; I should get it*. And then I forget about it until the next time I am in a store, or in someone's home, or watching a movie with a really good soundtrack, and I say to myself, *Oh, this is a good album; I should get it*. You see where I'm going with this. . . .

So, the reason why I bought this particular album is that I wanted to be supportive of the people who made it. It's the Dixie Chicks' *Taking the Long Way*, and I bought it because I want to support people who say what they think in the face of censure and disapproval.

I'm not a die-hard fan of the Dixie Chicks, but I was aware of the brouhaha they caused and the headlines they made when they, or at least one of them, announced at a concert in London (in response to President Bush's plans for a war in Iraq) that they were "ashamed the president of the United States is from Texas." This expression of their personal beliefs resulted in their suffering a whole slate of punishments, including appearance cancellations, being pulled from airplay, and, disturbingly, death threats. Despite all this, in the ensuing years they neither hid their heads in shame nor waged a campaign of apology; instead, they came out with an album that includes a song called "Not Ready to Make Nice" and won five Grammys, including Album of the Year. I can applaud that kind of backbone. And not only can I applaud it, I can support it.

It might have been me, but I often felt as if many of us were wandering through a cloud of confusion regarding the policies of the marathon Bush administration. There were moments of clarity, when people of stature called out for a little common sense when it came to invading a country with no real plan to speak of and then perpetuating a feeling of distrust and fear in our own country (a country, I should add, that should feel pretty good about its resources, abilities, and freedoms). Colin Powell was such a voice; but, sadly, he faded away into an immobilizing fog.

These sentiments were echoed in an ongoing discussion on a list-serv to which I belong. The Republicans in the group were immediately recognizable for their posts discussing support for the war and keeping immigrants illegal. Occasionally someone, presumably a Democrat, would respond with an argument citing the Iraq Study Group or *The Nation* or NPR or Iraq Veterans Against the War. The voracious response from those who disagreed was deafening. And then that old accusation surfaced: "That's just unpatriotic." Since when is taking advantage of freedom of speech unpatriotic? But voices espousing peace often disappear into the fog as if those of us against the war don't have a right to speak up. I am against the war—I am against all war—but I am not against those people who, in the commission of their jobs, are putting their very lives on the line. Frankly, I'd rather they have different jobs, but I am not against them, and I resent the suggestion that I need to support an unqualified war in order to be considered patriotic. I also resent the billions of dollars spent perpetuating such a war when we haven't taken care of a little problem called New Orleans. And I am incensed that our country—my country—treats people who come here from other countries as "illegal." I find the term as offensive as I do the policies denying such people the rights everyone who lives here is afforded.

But I'm not a political writer, and I probably won't be invited as a participant on a Sunday-morning talk show anytime soon. But I don't want to give up just because I don't think like a warmongering administration; I want to find a way to stop wandering in this fog of uncertainty and inaction. That's why I was so happy to purchase a CD made by a group that shows some backbone. I like seeing a bunch of women not buckle under pressure. I admire their attitude, and I admire the action they took in asserting their right to say what they felt they needed to say. I may still be wandering in the fog, looking for my own way not to buckle—but at least now I have a soundtrack.

Therapy, Maine-Style

It was bound to happen. I fled. I bolted. I put myself and my over-stressed life ahead of work, home, and duty and, knowing that my parents would be out of town at a friend's wedding in Vermont, hightailed it up to Maine. Knowing that I had Big Decisions to make and Big Plans to arrange. Gone. Outta here. Buh-bye. Husband and parents alike said, "Sure, Cindy, go ahead. That's fine." And I didn't wait around for second thoughts. I piled my books, DVDs, and comfy clothes in a bag and left right after work on Thursday.

I don't know what my problem was. Sure, life was feeling tough, but when doesn't it? But, like I said, I did have Big Decisions and Big Plans to make. My Big Decisions concerned my work/writing career—as in, *Do I continue to pretend I have a writing career, or should I just shut up and get a good, paying job?* The Big Plans had to do with my son's upcoming twenty-first birthday party. Annie and I were planning it. We were so excited! There was so much to do! So what was the first thing on my list? Fleeing. Tent rentals and a grilling menu would have to wait until the next week. Big help I turned out to be.

Here's what I did instead. . . .

Thursday Night

I arrive. I miss the 8:30 PM ferry by seconds. I watch it pull away from the gantry and start to make its turn toward the island. That's okay—I can wait a half hour. I'm here, so what's the rush now? It's dark in September at 8:30 PM; I can't see across the lake. But I know what's there. The ferry returns, allows me and a few others to board, and then, after a seven-and-a-half-minute ride, lets me off on the other side. The store is dark; the café has taken the tables off the lower deck, and they're piled up against the building for next year. There's a quiet to the island in the off-season that you can feel as soon as you've disembarked the ferry.

I drive down the dirt road with two cars behind me. When I reach the stop sign at the end of Sunset Road and turn left, I lose my last follower and continue on alone. The break in the trees at Cocktail Beach affords the first great view of the lake and the night sky glittering with stars. As I stared at them while I came across on the ferry, I thought how helpful it would be if I knew what I was looking at up there, all those lights arranged in such constant patterns. But I don't. I'm reminded of it again as I pass Cocktail Beach: so many stars, so little knowledge.

I pull up to the cottage. My mom left the kitchen light but none of the outside lights on. I leave the headlights aimed at the front door so I can get the door unlocked. I'm in. I tramp back to the car to put up windows and turn off lights and bring in the rest of my stuff. I don't have much. I plop it all down on the glider chair next to the fireplace, and that's pretty much where it will stay all weekend. I make the necessary "I made it safely" calls, pull on a sweatshirt and long pants (it's just the slightest bit chilly here), open a bottle of wine, and crack open the first of the three books I brought with me. Ahh.

Friday

I sleep like a baby when I'm here, but never late. This morning I was up at the break of dawn. It promised to be a beautiful day, the loveliest jewel in the Triple Crown of this weekend's days. I consider walking, swimming, or kayaking, and then give in to the pull that also got me last night: reading. I love reading. I never get to do it enough, though it's what I love to do the most. I'm an endomorph through and through, and my favorite pastime is to plop down on a chair in the sun, on a couch in front of a fire, or in the backseat of a moving car and read. This is what I do.

The sun is out, and it's warm and breezy. I wear shorts and a tank top even though it's just a tiny bit cool in the shade, which I avoid. It's the first day of my flee-dom, and I'm still trying to get comfortable with it. I forget to eat lunch (shocking), and I read until I need another cup of coffee around four. It occurs to me that engaging in some sort of activity would be a good thing, so I take my dad's walk at five o'clock. Every day he's been up here this year, he's taken his daily constitutional at around this time; I decide to continue the tradition while he's away. I take the "short walk," which leads out Island Road and down Leisure with a quick left on Harbor. (That's Harbor Road, not Harbor Lane. We are parsimonious up here on the island with our street names.) Harbor Lane is where I turn right and follow a short uphill back to Leisure and then a quick three-quarters of a mile back to Island and home. All in all it's about 1.2 miles, and it makes me feel as if I've done something physical besides lift my book up and put it down, lift it up and put it down, all day.

Saturday

Well, I knew this was coming—rain. Gray, cold, and rain wake me up, again at the crack of dawn, on this second day of flee-dom. If "saw" is the past tense of "see," is "flaw" the past tense of "flee"? Is it bad to ditch all my responsibilities and hide out for three days? I hope not, because that's what my intention is. It's been a rough summer. I've had enough. I'm tired and I'm done. I just want to be alone and read. Thank you, gray skies and cold drizzle, for providing the perfect backdrop to my misery.

I am halfway through book number two—a murder mystery, thank God, I couldn't take anything inspirational. I'm not going to walk today, obviously. It's raining. By 2:30 PM I'm done with my mystery (misery?), and I get up to shower, wash my hair, shave my legs, and generally just clean up. When I come out of the bathroom, there's light playing through the trees and making its way into the bedroom. What is this unexpected brightness? The sun? Outside, I see a little blue sky forcing its way across the lake above the White Mountains. The breeze picks up and the sun comes out, nearly blinding me. The brilliance is awesome; it shatters the gray water into bright bits of blue and gold. It is instantly beautiful. The air is clean, and I sit on the step of the wooden walkway to comb the knots out of my hair. Is this the same day? I spend about a half hour talking with my brother, Richard, about Sherlock Holmes and social networking and the latest celebrity news (because he lives in L.A.), letting the sun dry my hair and warm my chilled bones. Feels like a good pizza night, so I head down to the little store-café, order takeout, and bring it right back to the house.

The sunlight is still blazing across the lake. I pull the shade so I can watch one of the DVDs I brought: *The Professional*. I laugh, I cry, I fall asleep in the chair when it's over. Eventually I get up, turn off the TV, cap the wine bottle I opened but barely put a dent in, and turn off the lights. I bring book number three to bed with me, but I don't get very far into it. When I fall asleep this night, it's the rest of the weary: complete and nearly dreamless.

Sunday

The third day of desertion dawns with sunlight. My parents are returning today, but I don't know their time frame, and I am waiting for them to call. I'm feeling yesterday's lack of exercise, so, since I won't be around at the regular constitutional time, I set out for my final walk this morning. I always think I'll run into a moose or a bear here, but the only animal I see is a deer, who is as surprised to see me as I am to see it. Once back, I settle in to finish my reading and try to get some writing done. I will need to take the trash to the dump and tidy up a little before I go, although my imprint on the house this weekend has been minimal—as Goldilocks did, I tried out a few chairs, found the one I liked, and stayed there for the duration.

Book number three is a short one, and I take care of it in no time. Now I am left with Doing Some Writing. It was one of the reasons I came up here: to Write. As if I were a Writer. This is part of my Big Decision, so it weighs heavily on my mind, and I'm not too sure I want to tackle it in my newly relaxed and introspective mood, but I'll give it a shot. I try this topic and that topic, until I finally settle on . . . none of them. I close up my computer and turn my attention to trash and tidying.

The Drive Home

My parents never called, so all the way down the Maine Turnpike and most of the way through New Hampshire, I fret about their progress. Then my dad calls and says that they're at Hannaford for groceries. They didn't have cell service most of the way across Vermont and New Hampshire, and they'll be home in an hour or so. I'll miss them, but at least they'll get home safely. Whew.

A smile breaks across my face, finally. My three days of seclusion can at last settle into my psyche and go to work, like the relaxation part of a yoga class. The drive home allows all the weather and reading and walking and pizza and insights to find a place in which to nestle into my brain and body. I know I can't do it all the time, this fleeing from responsibility. But this time, a flaw was just what I needed.

A Monstrous Regiment
of Women

A little book called *Beavershots* fell into my hands today. Don't get too excited, boys—it's not what you think. At first glance, it is a recipe book filled with cute drawings of woodland beavers engaged in various activities and circumstances. Not one of them naked. The recipes it features are for beverages of the gelatin-and-pudding persuasion. It's quite informative, and well equipped, too, as it comes with its own blue mesh sleeve of tiny plastic cups and lids. I am assuming this is how one makes gelatin shots. (As I am fifty-something, gelatin shots are not included in my drinking repertoire. Consider that my alcoholic-beverage references include Nickel Beer Night, and you'll get my drift.)

So, at first glance, as I noted, it's a recipe book. It is filled, however, with hysterically—some, including me, might say disturbingly—named tiny-drink recipes. Can I say right now that I am unhappy that shockingly named drinks disturb me? This is totally an age thing, and I have no control in the matter. I first noticed it when Sex on the Beach cocktails became popular, and I was shocked and appalled—first at the name, then at my reaction.

But I digress.

Upon reading past the incredibly manageable ingredient lists, I found that this book was created by a group of women. Not just one—or, even worse, some guy and an advertising agency—but a real, down-to-earth, red-blooded, hardworking group of women friends. I know this because I read the back of the book and because I know one of the women who wrote it. The woman, Deb, is someone I used to work with. She is a teacher and is raising three children. She also holds down a second job but still manages to find the time to build furniture and hang out with her friends. And it's within this group of friends that she apparently finds her store of strength. When she came by my house to drop off the book, she was on her way to IKEA during the latest nor'easter with her three kids in tow. I cleaned up the remnants from the waffle sticks and cups of milk that had comprised the morning's breakfast and considered how on earth she managed to fit in writing a book with all she does. And then I considered that Deb's life may be full of the demands of teaching, child rearing, and bartending (her second job—makes sense, right?), but she also draws upon the strength of women—a formidable force indeed.

Beavershots was not the only book I read that week. I also had the privilege of reading a friend's master's thesis, which detailed the path of her life from the first blush of love to the pain and torture of love gone bad. Along the way, she had to make decisions with long-lasting consequences for her family, and she made them according to her own beliefs rather than according to what society and general consensus would consider proper. Or reasonable. Or sane. Many of her decisions and actions took her far from the path of "When I grow up, I want to be a wife and a mommy" and led her to places where she had no instruction booklet to guide her. I know this because I went to those places during the crumbling of my own storybook marriage. These decisions are made not from courage, but from fear. Or, as Eddie Rickenbacker once said, "Courage is doing what you're afraid to do. There can be no courage unless you're scared."

The power of women is a subtle strength that feeds our society at its most basic level, and yet it is overlooked time and time again.

This past week, reading these two books, I realized once again how deeply women reach for their strength, and it flung me back on my heels. On the surface, one was a book of cheeky advice on how to have a great party and the other was written to satisfy a requirement for a degree, but if you scratch below the surface, you can see how both give evidence to the depths and the breadths women will go to to reach their goals, help their friends, care for their children, and live their lives.

How blithely it is assumed that we will do what is necessary—and yet how quickly that very behavior is minimized and diminished in labels like "feminazis" and "ball breakers" when it is convenient. Need proof? Three words: Hillary Rodham Clinton.

This is not a political stance; this is a love letter to women I know—to their strength and to their persistence and to their courage. I've mentioned only two, but as I consider the other women in my life through this newly discovered lens, I realize what an amazing discovery this is. The scary part is that I belong to this club. I have a lot to live up to.

Impostor

When I was a teenager, from about age thirteen to seventeen-ish, I retreated into the world of old movies. This was before the advent of cable, boys and girls—back in the day of a thirteen-inch black-and-white television with rabbit ears and a channel dial that I actually had to get up from my bed to change. I had my choice of three, maybe four stations after 11:00 PM. My parents didn't need to concern themselves with the dire "It's eleven o'clock. Do you know where your children are?" warning; I was upstairs, watching TV. Clark Gable, Greer Garson, Joan Fontaine, Cary Grant—these were my late-night buddies, the people with whom I had tons in common and from whom I tried to divine some knowledge about how to manage my awkward life during the day.

One movie I remember in particular is *The Great Impostor*, which starred Tony Curtis as Fred Demara, the famous pretender. To this day, all I can recall from the entire movie is the tension I felt as I watched it, worried that he might get caught. I was so anxious about it that I couldn't enjoy the movie. And I continue to have that feeling as an adult: I'm an impostor, and I can't believe I haven't been caught. I'm almost fifty, and I've pulled off some of the greatest hoaxes of the century (centuries, to be accurate, since I've spanned the twentieth and twenty-first).

I'm not sure when I got my first taste of pretending, but it was probably back in high school, where I pretended I knew what the hell I was doing. People I went to school with probably recall me as smiling and happy—not popular, but certainly social enough to show up at some of the parties and basketball games. They don't know most of my trusted friends at the time lived in a tiny, faux-wood-grained box on my dresser at night.

I did essentially the same thing at college, except that there I abandoned my *Late Night at the Movies* friendships for my room-mate, Sue. She had an abundance of confidence and guts, and I pretended I could keep up with her in her escapades. When it got too scary, I would claim a headache or a paper to write and would stay in our room while everyone else went out to the Austin Hill Country for a concert or to Lake Travis for a picnic on a boat with some cool guys we had met at the Bucket on Nickel Beer Night. Nickel Beer Night, I could manage; boys on boats were way out of my league.

I guess one of my earliest successful hoaxes was becoming a wife at age twenty-one. That took some doing, as I needed to dupe my husband, my family, and my friends. I was the first one of anyone I knew to get married, so my only real experience to draw on was my parents' marriage. But they figured I knew what I was doing—prob-ably since I had done my best impersonation of a young woman in love who had taken everything into consideration and planned and pulled off an August wedding in Texas. (Although who plans an August wedding in Texas but an impostor? Shouldn't that have been a big, fat clue?)

Then came parenting. What does a twenty-two-year-old who just became a wife know about having a baby? I'll tell you: noth-ing. Fortunately, my baby was not an impostor, and she knew what she was doing. And an equally knowledgeable son came after her. Anything I did right in the parenting department was just dumb luck. Just like when Tony Curtis/Fred Demara, pretending to be a doctor, successfully performs dental surgery on the captain of the destroyer he is serving on. Whew!

Little successes over the years did nothing for my confidence;

they only exacerbated the fear that I would be found out. So I would ratchet up my nerves and keep going—taking jobs, leaving one marriage and entering another, raising my kids, going back to school, buying a house, and getting involved in any number of other crazy adventures I had no business undertaking, because I'm an impostor and I have no idea what I'm doing.

One weekend, I went to a writing retreat with a bunch of other writing women. It was both comfortable and intimidating, because there, too, I felt like an imposter. Even doing the one thing I know I can do, the one thing I love so much and can't imagine not having in my life—writing—I felt I was an interloper, a fake, in the company of so much talent and realness. But then, as one after another of us read from her journal after writing for a specified time, that feeling changed. The words hovering in the room were powerful and strong—they were the words of women who had struggled their whole lives against the conditions and expectations others set upon them. Fear and pain, doubt and hope, desire and longing, frustration and censure—all were contained within the experience of the women with whom I wrote that day. Maybe I was an impostor, but I was in the company of those who could know that they had an impostor in their midst and still be welcoming.

I put my foot outside my front door every day and walk toward the world feeling the weight of responsibility and truth. I do the best job I can, and when I return home at the end of the day, I don't always know that I've done anything at all. That's the life of the impostor, I suppose. There's anxiety, and there's uncertainty. But there's hope, too, the hope that comes, as it did in that room full of women writers, when I learn something in spite of—and perhaps even as a result of—all my posing.

The Anti-Tourist

For many who live in one of the more affluent suburbs of New York City (I'm speaking of Connecticut, of course), the annual trip into "the City" for Christmas shopping is de rigueur. I've known people to take sick days in order to complete this most required of preholiday activities, just so that they can say, upon their return, "Oh, yes, I picked that up in the City" and further impress friends and family with their deeply felt sense of Christmas. During this time, the train station parking lots in Brewster and various points south are filled to capacity with Highlanders, Suburbans, and Odysseys bearing Connecticut license plates. It's not that surprising, then, upon making that first and urgent stop in the ladies' room at Grand Central, to hear conversations about "the horrendous traffic on 84" (the congestion-snarled interstate that bisects Connecticut), nor to see said conversants file out and head en masse to Rockefeller Center, where they will watch the skaters, pick up some treats at Dean & DeLuca, and fan out to support all manner of trendy and overpriced stores, boutiques, and restaurants.

It's enough to make you throw up.

A couple of years ago, I made just such a pilgrimage to the City. On a Friday morning, I drove to the Southeast Train Station, just north of Brewster (a much better station than the one in Brewster—there's tons of parking, it's easy to get to, and there's a Dunkin Donuts a mile away), and got on the train.

I almost decided not to go at the last minute. A quick snow-storm the night before had dumped several inches of snow, which had turned quickly to slush, onto the roads and into the parking lots—and I'd worn my FUGGS (that's shorthand for "faux UGGs," for those of you ignorant of fashion knockoffs) with a hole in the bottom of the right shoe. My sock was wet for the whole train ride down—it would dry just in time, I figured, to get drenched again when I got off the train and started walking around the City. I didn't turn back, though; I persevered.

Once settled in on the train, I realized I had been looking for reasons not to go since the morning prior: the weather, the crowds, the expense, the fear, the inability to find my way around all by myself. Usually I retain an excellent sense of direction and can find my way around anywhere, but for some reason, when I am in the City I get disoriented just walking in and out of Bed Bath & Beyond. (This admission is usually when I hear the exasperated "It's a grid! The avenues go north and south, and the streets go east and west!" Duh. Does this mean I can't enjoy a moment of reconnaissance for a minute here?) Anyway, as I sat on the train, the possibility that I'd end up in Harlem instead of Chelsea was a real concern for me. On the pro side of the inner argument I continued with myself, how-ever, was the fact that I needed to expand my realm of reference. How could I be a writer and not be able to go into New York all by myself? I needed to get out there, do things beyond my comfort zone, put myself in danger—and if fighting a bunch of ladies and children wearing real UGGs for a stall in the Grand Central Station ladies' room isn't dangerous, I don't know what is. So off I went.

The first *you did the right thing, Cindy* moment happened right in the ladies' room. I walked right in, no waiting. As I held my hands under the hand dryer, I noticed that where there once had been no line, a serpentine queue was now snaking outside the door.

Ha! I beat you! I beat you all!

Hopefully I didn't say that out loud. I walked past the line of scowling ladies and out through the terminal—not stopping to glance at the ceiling's light show, which would peg me as an outsider in a second. I walked to the closest door and went outside. It was cold and sunny, and all eight million City inhabitants were on the street . . . but there was no slush! I started walking as if I knew where I was going. I knew where I wanted to go, but I had to call Annie so she could help me get my bearings.

Gotta love cell phones; gotta love them even more when the person you're calling answers. "I'm on Madison Avenue and Forty-Third—which way do I go to get to Rockefeller Center?" I asked her. I know what you're thinking: *She's such a tourist, heading right to where everyone else is going.* But I had another destination in mind.

Annie gave me directions and I started off, west on Forty-Third and then north on Fifth Avenue, until I found what I was looking for. Not the skating rink or the crowds trying to catch a glimpse of themselves on the *Today* show, but the Penny Harvest, part of an annual educational program that teaches students about fighting hunger. I was carrying a Ziploc bag with about three pounds of pennies in it, and I needed to get them to this block-long piggy bank before I could go on with my adventure.

I tossed the pennies in a few at a time to prolong the experience, wishing there were a couple of kids there whom I could share the penny pitching with. One of the attendants told me I had just missed a busload of second graders. I could just imagine the looks on their faces when encountering this ginormous field of copper. I'm sure my own face reflected the same amazement.

From there I started walking south on Fifth Avenue—on the sunny side of the street, of course. As I passed Forty-Second Street, I realized I was coming up on the New York Public Library. It is such an imposing building, sitting there daring people to ignore Banana Republic and come in for some quiet and culture. I took the dare and walked up the stone steps and into the cavernous lobby. I had never been inside before, and I figured I would be met by the sight of thousands and thousands of books on dark oak shelves, but it was only a lobby with staircases to the left and right and a sign over a door announcing an exhibit—*The Beatific Soul: Jack Kerouac on the Road*. I didn't have any bags to check, so I turned off my cell phone and went in.

The exhibit hall held dozens of glass cases in which Jack's crisp, precise writing covered pages and pages of notebooks. There were black-and-white photographs of him, William S. Burroughs, Allen Ginsberg, and others. (Who knew Jack was so handsome?) The quiet of the hall drew me in farther and farther. I wandered slowly around the cases and displays. Toward the end, I saw examples of his graphic-arts ability in the baseball cards he'd made up (color-coded!). His "newspaper" had a masthead and columns, drawn with precision in pencil.

I decided against taking a brochure. The experience was already embedded in my soul; no paper-and-ink souvenir would make it any more significant. I sat outside the library at a green metal bistro table and took out my journal. I watched the other people walk back and forth on Fifth Avenue, laden with shopping bags, cell phones, and paper coffee cups, feeling as if I didn't have anything in common with them but at the same time that I wasn't an outsider, either. I wasn't a resident, but I wasn't a tourist. I was the Anti-Tourist, avoiding the doorways of the brand names lying in wait for me and my money. They were too late. I'd already dumped my money into the world's biggest penny jar.

I sat for a few more minutes before setting off again. I didn't have anything left to do besides meet up with Annie and Tony later so we could head back together on the train. I reluctantly left my chair and vantage point to continue walking down Fifth Avenue. I still needed to get myself west to Annie and Tony's apartment, but for now I kept on walking south.

The literary air of the library wrapped around me like a warm scarf and kept me from getting in line behind the brass poles and velvet ropes a couple of blocks south. Was this a line to visit Santa? Were these people patient patrons waiting for a seat at a fancy restaurant? Nope. The line I came upon was for those who wished to see the festively decorated windows of the Lord & Taylor department store. Can you believe it? A line to see windows! New Yorkers will line up to see anything! As you might suppose, one can actually see the windows beyond the velvet ropes. But I guess it's more of an event if you wait your turn to get in line and then walk slowly behind another tourist with your digital camera, only to find out after you've downloaded your pictures to your computer that your flash has obliterated the scene you waited for so long to capture. I smiled at these silly tourists, dug my hands into my pockets, adjusted my shades, and kept walking.

By this point I was feeling quite comfortable, grid or no grid. I wasn't worried I would get lost, or turned around, or snatched into a waiting van and forced into some dark world of white slavery. (Oh, didn't I mention I might have been a tad concerned about that?) All at once, I was a citizen of the City. It was my city, too, and I could go anywhere—or not. I was unafraid and energized. I didn't have to follow the hordes of tourists out of Grand Central Station and, like a lemming, jump off the cliff into the Hard Rock Café or Radio City Music Hall. I could walk downtown to the beat of a different drummer—sit for a minute in one of the parks, or poke through one of the street-vendor stalls that sit on every corner. And if I didn't like the drummer on Fifth Avenue, I could always walk down the long block west to Sixth Avenue, and there would be another one there. I could go where I liked. Screw the grid.

4:00 AM

It wasn't any o'clock in the morning that I wanted to be up. Some mornings, when you suddenly wake up at 3:51 AM, it's because you need to go to the bathroom or get a drink of water; it takes all of three and a half minutes, and you're back in bed before 3:55 AM.

That particular morning started out like this: I was sufficiently sleepy to be pretty certain I'd be back to dreaming in no time; I got all settled into my pillow, flung the blankets off to my husband's side of the bed, and waited for sweet sleep to overtake me once again. But sweet sleep wasn't paying attention. Sweet sleep had already moved on to easier prey. There I was, waiting, my eyes wide open, but nothing was happening. I knew I was in trouble when I heard the town hall clock tower ring out: *bong . . . bong . . . bong . . . bong.* Four AM, and I was nowhere near going back to sleep.

I once heard a tip for times like these. When you have a million things swirling around in your head and you can't sleep because you're thinking of everything you need to get done, the best thing to do is to get up, find a pad of paper, and make yourself a list. Once you've acknowledged all the turmoil and created a neat little to-do list that will be ready for you when you wake back up, you should be able to go back to sleep. I'd done it before, and it had always seemed to do the trick. I might as well do it again. So I decided to get up, and I headed downstairs so as not to wake up my husband, who was sleeping quite soundly because I had so thoughtfully added extra blankets to his side of the bed.

Once downstairs, I looked for the cat. We'd had her for a little over six months at that point—we had adopted her when we were in Maine, closing the cottage, the October prior. We'd seen a local news story about the enormous population of cats and kittens left at the Portland Animal Shelter during the summer months; they were holding a clearance sale on cats older than two years of age, no adoption fee. We felt we had properly mourned our last cat, Chloe (God rest her soul), and it was time. We were ready for a new addition to the family.

To make a long story short (am I ever able to do that?), we browsed the shelter for about an hour and a half before finally settling on Valerie—who, we read in her most recent exit interview, was fearful, not playful, and liked going outside. We chose her because it also said she was fastidious and clean. We like that in a cat. And also because she was pretty: all black, with big green eyes matching the color of our house.

It took us about a week to discover that our new pet was a better Maia than a Valerie, and that she was one of the most affectionate, playful, and brainy cats we had ever met. We worried about her going out, but she insisted, so we relented and put in a cat door so she could come in and out at will—but only until 9:00 PM. As the weather got warmer, though, she pushed us to adjust her original curfew. We indulged her, as is typical with the last child, until we found a pile of her fur on our front porch one morning. The remnants of a neighborhood catfight, no doubt. "Back to 9:00 PM!" we said. "No way!" she argued, and has stayed out later and later each night since.

And so, since I was up anyway, at 4:15 AM. I went to see if I could induce her to come inside.

When I opened the back porch door, there she was, sleeping on the bench next to the railing. I softly called her name; she roused, and I could see her looking around in the predawn dark.

She jumped down from the bench, and I called to her again, holding the door open. She walked in a little circle, looking at me and then back at her perch. Then she just stayed still. For a split second I thought I had mistaken her for one of the neighborhood cats. Then she walked toward me a little, stopped, looked around again as if to get her bearings, and finally came in the door. I went to sit at my computer, and she looked at me as if to say, *Why did you make me come in? I wasn't doing anything wrong* (as last children are wont to declare). She stared at the closed door for a few minutes, until, realizing I had put my foot down, she finally jumped up on the chair across from me and promptly fell asleep. Cats, it seems, do not need to make to-do lists in order to get back to sleep.

I turned on my computer and fiddled around with some schedules for a program I was going to run the next week, looked at a couple of other lists I'd made, and sent off my résumé for another job posting. I wondered what the recipients would think about my having submitted my application at 4:45 AM. *Do we want this nut job at our place of business?* Judging from the lack of responses to the other half dozen or so applications I'd submitted in the last few months, the answer was no.

I checked my email. Lots of special offers and great deals had arrived in my inbox during the early-morning hours, but nothing to relieve the stress and anxiety I was feeling, so I shut everything down and headed back upstairs to see if sweet sleep had made it back to my bedroom.

As I waited, I thought of Maia wandering around the porch earlier, and it reminded me of what my thinking had been like lately. I was in a familiar place, but the anxious thoughts keeping me up were just wandering around and around, offering no clarity. I had so many things to do, so many decisions to make, but I just couldn't decide what to do. Like I was peering through the predawn dark, I could see them, and I knew I had to address them, but I just couldn't perceive them clearly enough to know what to do about any of it. Should I quit my job and trust that the universe would scoop me up and provide another one? Could I cobble together enough part-time jobs so as not to become a foreclosure statistic?

I realized that, like Maia, I just needed to wake up and go inside, and everything would be fine. Waking up was unpleasant, but I could just go back to sleep somewhere else. Not literally, of course. It's a tough place to be, this dark dawn before the light—but if a cat can handle it, I suppose I can, too.

Uninsured

I emailed this quote to my friend Laura one day:

"Until one is committed, there is hesitancy, the chance to draw back, always ineffectiveness. Concerning all acts of initiative (and creation), there is one elementary truth the ignorance of which kills countless ideas and splendid plans: that the moment one definitely commits oneself, then providence moves, too. A whole stream of events issues from the decision, raising in one's favor all manner of unforeseen incidents, meetings and material assistance, which no man could have dreamt would have come his way. I learned a deep respect for one of Goethe's couplets:

'Whatever you can do or dream you can, begin it.
Boldness has genius, power and magic in it!' "
—W. H. Murray, *The Scottish Himalaya Expedition*

Back in the day, this quote was hanging on my bathroom wall. I had printed it out on pretty, sparkly paper and taped it above the towel rack next to the sink. It had "spoken" to me, and I wanted to keep it around always. What better place to have a daily reminder than in the bathroom? Certainly not the closet, where I kept the ironing board.

The first time I quit my job without having a neat plan in the wings, I used that quote on the homemade thank-you notes that I sent to people who supported my decision with inspirational cards and messages. No money, though. Not a one sent me so much as a gift certificate to the grocery store or a discreet twenty-dollar bill tucked inside the envelope. The church staff did have a nice luncheon for me on my last day, however. After a delightful meal, they presented me with a lovely pewter bowl, thereby assuring that I would, at least, have a pot to piss in.

I don't have a distinct memory of how I handled the "What about health insurance?" question, so it must not have been a huge consideration for me at the time. Both of my kids were covered under their father's plan, so it was just me who had to stay healthy and out of the way of falling objects or icy sidewalks. I was a mere thirty-seven years old—I was still bulletproof. Quite honestly, I was more worried about keeping a roof over our heads and occasionally putting food on the table. No big deal. Bulletproof.

Thirteen years later, same boat, bigger waves. I had quit my job for reasons of integrity and passion. Pretty noble stuff. Only this time, I *was* concerned about health insurance. Because it wasn't just me who needed it; my former plan covered my husband, too. And just to drive that point home, my back went out less than forty-eight hours after my coverage ended. But wait—it gets funnier. Next I suffered an attack of pain, which I decided could be attributed only to a golf ball–size kidney stone that I was about to pass—and the day after that, my husband felt a sudden and never-before-experienced sharp pain begin to course through his left knee. I raised my eyes heavenward and shouted, "This isn't funny!" But my shouting was to no avail. The pain didn't stop, and my worrying about it seemed to only exacerbate it—the catch-22 of the uninsured.

The backache, I reasoned, could be one of those tests I hate so much. I've never been a good test-taker. In fact, I am terrible at it. And this test was no different, except that this must be one of those "in life the lesson comes after the test" tests. Ugh. The trick must be to carry on through the pain. Was I going to wimp out and run to the doctor or the pharmacist every time a little ache or bump got me down? What was I, some big, whiny baby? (Well, sometimes.) But really, was I going to let a little thing like excruciating agony keep me from reaching my goals?

The right answer—which this time I knew—was "No!" *With* the exclamation point. It's true that our country is sadly lacking in providing adequate health care coverage for its citizens, but that shouldn't be a factor in whether a person gets to do the kind of work that he or she finds meaningful, satisfying, and rewarding. It's kind of criminal, really, when you think about it. Not only has our society allowed the insurance companies to make decisions regarding our treatment—when, how often, with whom, and where—but it also prevents us from making the kind of quality-of-life decisions that are crucial to our becoming productive and contributing members of our communities. I may end up looking like Goldie Hawn or Meryl Streep at the end of the movie *Death Becomes Her*, but I know—even though the unfairness of it all makes me angry sometimes—that I just have to keep going.

So I sent the quote off to Laura because it had come up in a discussion we'd had the day prior. We had just been to a poetry reading and were feeling inspired. We had also just been to a Whole Foods Market and were feeling totally organic and healthy, having bought lots of natural and expensive food items. We talked about all this stuff—meaningful work, making choices, the occasional aches and pains—and I remembered the words that had started my days years earlier, and I told her I'd send them to her. Because this is what those words always said to me: *You think you're ready to make this bold move? Go ahead, but prepare to be tested. Take this! And that! . . . Still committed? We'll see.* And then Providence lends a hand.

Missing Elizabeth

Death puts things in perspective. Any arguments I may have with my husband seem to pale in the face of how much time we may or may not have here on Earth and how we spend our time together.

Elizabeth was one of three friends I had in high school. I don't remember how we even became friends—and, upon reflection, it's difficult to fathom that we did. She lived in "old Louisville," down by Mockingbird Valley and the Louisville Country Club, and my family was a recent transplant to one of the new, cookie-cutter subdivisions built on farmland out Old Brownsboro Road. Elizabeth was the very first preppie I ever met. She wore pink and green all the time. Or navy skirts patterned with tiny whales or pineapples, topped with polo shirts with the collar flipped up. And on her feet, always, were the slim, color-coordinated Pappagallo shoes she favored.

I liked it best when she came over to my house. When I went to her house, which I remember as a weathered old brick colonial with multi-paned windows and winding stairways shaded by twenty-foot trees that let in only slivered glimpses of sunlight, I felt like an unsophisticated bumpkin from the sticks. Upstairs, on our way to her room, we'd go through a cluttered foyer strewn with toys and books and clothes and pillows. I'd never been in such a house before. All the houses in our neighborhood were brand-new, with fresh paint and shoe box–size rooms, and they sat on lots with spindly new trees and gravel driveways.

At Elizabeth's house, one or another of her four brothers and sisters was always getting ready to be taken to the club for tennis or swimming or some other activity requiring special clothes. I rarely saw her father. I often saw her mother. I was never as intimidated by a friend's mom as I was by hers. And Elizabeth referred to her mother as Bonnie. Who did that? Not anyone I knew. I always felt I must carry some faint, unpleasant scent with me because of the way her mom kept her distance from me. To be fair, she was never unkind; I just wasn't *her* kind. Plus, she was managing a family of seven while keeping perfectly coiffed and attired. I'm not sure this is accurate, but in my memory she always wore a string of pearls, like June Cleaver.

With Elizabeth, I went to high school parties for whose guest list my name wasn't even a consideration and hung out with people who normally wouldn't even have glanced my way in the hallways. It was exhilarating and scary for a bumpkin, but it was as easy as breathing for Elizabeth.

I got word of Elizabeth's death through the high school listserv that has continued since our thirtieth reunion in 2006. Elizabeth didn't attend the reunion, though I hoped she would. I had lost touch with her many years earlier, sometime after I left the Atlanta area, where we both lived for a short time when my daughter was about one. That had been the only thing that made our move to Atlanta the least bit positive for me—the fact that I would be able to reconnect with Elizabeth. We lived in a big house in Alpharetta, some twenty miles or so from Atlanta. Since I was a married stay-at-home mom and she was a single working girl, we didn't hang out too often, but she would come over for dinner sometimes and stay over rather than drive all the way back into town at night.

One of my most vivid memories is of watching her get ready to leave in the morning. I was always up early because of Annie, but Elizabeth got up early, too—to begin her morning regimen. First there was her bath. Not a shower, a bath. With bubbles. After bathing, she would hoist her toiletry case (the size of my whole overnight bag) onto the counter and begin the magic. Hair, makeup, clothes. I never knew a person could spend that kind of time in the bathroom. (Except my daughter—who, now that I think about it, may have been strongly impacted by Elizabeth's ministrations as we sat on the toilet seat watching her each morning. She's exactly the same way.)

We lost touch after several years of birthday cards and occasional letters. I heard she moved to Colorado at one point, and every so often, with the advent of the Internet and search engines, I would try and locate her whereabouts. When plans for the reunion produced the email listserv, I checked in to see if she had signed up, but she was one of the ones who was listed as "not found." At the reunion I asked a few people if they knew where she was, but no one seemed to know. I suppose the easiest way would have been to contact her parents, but there was no urgency to my search; who would have thought she'd be gone in just a few short years?

I thought of Elizabeth a lot in the weeks after I found out about her death. I dreamed about her at night. I scoured my attic boxes for old pictures of her. From the few people who responded to the obituary via email, I found out that she had suffered from a chronic illness as a result of an accident years earlier and had died at home in Atlanta, far from the friends who obviously loved her in Aspen.

In my need to find out who Elizabeth had become over the years, I contacted one of the people who posted an online condolence on the newspaper's "Legacy" website. Despite his own grief at losing a friend, he graciously responded and described his friend Elizabeth to me in much the way I remembered her: beautiful, generous, caring, and loving. And even though it's been over twenty-five years, I miss her. I can picture her laughing and talking and having a good time with whoever she happened to be with at the moment. Her friendship gave me confidence and entrée into a social world I never would have been accepted into without her as my envoy. I miss knowing the woman she grew into, and I miss her not knowing the beautiful young woman my daughter, Suzanne Elizabeth, has become.

Missing Elizabeth has given me a new perspective on life—and if that sounds trite or maudlin, so be it. How many times must I lose a friend or family member only to let my commitment to be more conscious of what's dear to me fade away with my grief? I'm really not that old, and neither was Elizabeth. I never thought there was a time limit on how long I could think, *I wonder what Elizabeth is doing*, do a quick Google search, come up empty, and eventually forget about it. Somewhere in my heart, I always felt I'd find her one day and we'd make a plan to meet, catch up, laugh, and cry, and promise to stay in touch. Now we can't. I don't even know if she ever felt the same way, or if she remembered me in the same way in which I remember her. But a little part of her is with me now, even after all these years. I'll always be grateful for her friendship and what it continues to mean to me—even as I am missing her now.

Two Hours Later . . .

What in the world did I do before the Internet and cell phones? With my time, I mean. Right now I am sitting on my porch on a gorgeous Sunday morning, bees buzzing, birds chirping. A softball game's cheers echo in the distance, and there are two-foot-high weeds growing before my very eyes. I've got my cell phone by my side and a laptop on my lap. Maybe when I sat down a couple of hours ago, it was to do a little writing and order some castile soap that I can't get in my local stores, but at this point I've visited my Facebook page and logged in to my Blogger site, checked the weather in Maine for our trip next week (rain—what a shock), and read up on Niagara Falls and the Erie Canal. I've written a letter to the president of the college where I teach and checked my email, both personal and work. I've texted Annie to let her know we received a thank-you note from her friend, and will be waiting to hear via cell phone from my husband about his grill search and my son about his ETA at home. So I ask again: What in the world did I do on a Sunday morning—or any other day, at any other time—before the Internet and cell phones?

It would seem as though I must have gotten a lot more done in my life before these technologies entered it, but I don't feel as though I'm doing less of anything. My clothes are clean, there is food in the house, and the electricity hasn't been turned off. The work I'm doing is getting done with the same effort and outcomes as I used to achieve. Maybe I did a little more reading before. Maybe that's what I would have been doing, say, ten years ago, with a gorgeous morning at my disposal. I sure didn't do anything athletic, that's for sure. I didn't—and don't—run or jog or bike, so it's not like I've given up anything particularly healthy. Or outdoorsy. Although sitting on my porch technically qualifies as being "outdoors."

The thing is, I love the Internet and cell phones, I love the instant-information capabilities of the Internet, and I love the anytime/anywhere contact that cells allow. A perfect example: My husband and I drove up to Canada to do a presentation at a conference a while back, and as we drove across the state of New York, I noticed a body of water running parallel to the highway. "Is that the Erie Canal?" I asked. Angelo wasn't sure either, so we opened up our laptop at the next rest area, logged on to the Wi-Fi provided there, and found out that, yes, it was. And it was kind of cool to know that that's what we were driving by. We also used the opportunity to register the E-ZPass we'd picked up while we were at the service center (the toll is a whopping fifteen bucks by the time you get to the end of the New York State Thruway), so we were able to go on our merry way, the money in our pockets now available for Starbucks coffee and Tim Horton's bagels instead of the toll collectors. As we approached Buffalo, I sent a text to our kids and family to let them know that we wouldn't be calling much once we crossed the border, since international calls and texts cost more—but just in case, I used my cell to call our carrier and add an international calling plan to our service. Just like that.

So, yep, I love the Internet and cell phones. But do they take up—or waste—too much of my time? I don't know. But I love being able to get the information I want on any given topic or question in an instant. What did I do before when I heard about something I wanted to know more about, like a new restaurant or little-known facts about a historic canal? Went to a library, I guess, or waited for the next day's newspaper—and in the meantime, maybe I cleaned something or raised a child or read a book. I'll be the first to admit that I can get lost once I pop open the cover of my laptop to "just look up this one thing" or "check my email real quick." Poof!—I'm gone, and suddenly the sun has set or it's too late to make risotto or the bank is closed. And I've spent another couple of hours online, with nothing to show for it but an empty spam folder. So maybe I should attack those toddler-size weeds instead of checking my inbox one more time. Nothing is going to happen in the next few hours that can't wait until later, or even tomorrow morning. And if it does, I can always read about it online.

Picture Perfect

A fter Annie's wedding, there was a definite absence of chaos—the good kind of chaos—and both my daughter and I experienced a kind of letdown, much like what you experience after you finish performing in a play or giving birth to a child. But my post-wedding depression was quickly replaced by anxiety, because then we were waiting for the photographer to send us the pictures from the event.

Early posts from a few relatives and friends on Facebook revealed my daughter to be the most beautiful bride ever and her husband to be equally handsome. They looked like they could be on the cover of *Bride* or *Martha Stewart Weddings*. My new best friend, Sue (mother of the groom, or MOTG), had already put up a new profile picture of herself from the wedding on Facebook as well, one of her smiling into the camera mid-dance with her husband. It was charming—a great picture of them both.

And then there were the few shots of me. Who let me out of the house looking like that? Not that it was all about me, but really. I dreaded the album about to land in our family photographic history. I was sure that none of the pictures would reflect the "me" I imagined I looked like. Now *that* was depressing.

When I got dressed for the wedding, I glanced in the mirror and thought, *Hmm. Not bad.* My husband concurred. I looked at myself head-on and sideways, and I felt like going out in public the way

I looked was reasonable. And there was a guest at the wedding, a friend of the bride and groom, from Miami—about five foot seven, blonde hair, very pretty and friendly, wearing a smart little black dress with a pale taupe shawl over it—and I thought to myself when I saw her, *Hmm, we could be twins.* I actually think I look like this when I go out in public.

Now, sadly, I had photographic evidence to the contrary. In dozens of pictures on who knows how many Facebook walls, Snapfish accounts, Picasa pages, cell phones, digital cameras, and laptops of the 150 people present at the wedding, there I was, dispelling my personal myth of what I look like. If that's not cause to call my therapist, I don't know what is.

Again, I know it's not all about me. Annie and Tony will go through their wedding pictures over and over during the next several decades, and doing so will bring them joy and happiness. And the dress I wore—my wedding dress from when I married my husband eight years ago—is beautiful. On the hanger, anyway. On me it looked like someone had wrapped an apartment-size refrigerator in light saffron silk with a gold-lace overlay and rolled it down the aisle with my daughter. My shoes were nice, though, and they really did look like I'd imagined them to look, even on me. When I'm forced to relive this event in the years to come, I suppose I can simply focus on my feet.

I suspect that I am not the only woman in America who thinks of herself this way. In fact, I'm pretty sure the fashion industry counts on that. Why else would they sell black leggings in size XXL? That's not right. But do I buy them? Yep. Not the XXL ones, granted, but I definitely am more comfortable in L than in M. I usually cover them up with a tunic to conceal the more bulgy parts of my body, but still, after I consult my mirror and see my delusional perception of myself reflected back at me, I usually go right out the front door and into the public eye. Where people can see me. I don't think I scare young children, but maybe their parents have already hurried them out of my path before I've noticed any of their horrified faces.

I know what you're thinking: *Hey, Cin, why not just start running?* or *Try that great new Mediterranean diet*. Et cetera. Et cetera. First of all, I've seen runners running. They look like they're having the worst, most excruciating experience of their lives. No thanks. I take the stairs when I can and eat a healthy diet. Mostly. The thing is, it's not like I need to "get back to when I was thinner." I was never thinner. I can't grow another five inches taller (though that would do wonders for my other delusion, the height-weight chart on the label of the tights I always buy). Of course, the big clue here is that I always buy *black* tights. Sure, I could make a concerted effort to lose some weight. But even then, I'm pretty sure, I still wouldn't be able to reconcile the me in my head with the me in photographs. I would still be . . . me.

I know this is not just my problem. I've seen those women exposing their midriffs in tight jeans and cropped tops. They have muffin tops, and they go out in public. They don't have a problem scaring young children. Either they think, like I do, that they are the spitting image of Jennifer Aniston or they think that the roll of fat hanging over the waistline of their jeans is sexy. Or maybe they just don't think about it at all and are simply happy with who they are and what they look like.

Now there's a concept.

My Bad (Day)

One morning, in honor of my decision to write every Tuesday and Thursday, I got up early. I made a quick bowl of oatmeal and had a neat shot of espresso (I know, you thought I was going to say scotch). I had no classes, no visits, no appointments—just time for me, me, me. And I had an idea for an essay to write. But first I wanted to reduce at least one of the four piles of crap that obscured all the open space on my desk.

My home office used to be planted in the middle of our living room. Which worked just fine until we had company or someone wanted to watch TV or any number of other small and large distractions that keep one from getting any work done at home reared their heads. For instance, the office's proximity to the kitchen. Now, I've got a whole room. And I've got a desk—one with drawers and everything. It became my desk when my husband and I decided that he had all the office space he needed in the building where our mom-and-pop therapy business is. The room at home, which he used to use, was declared mine: he moved out most of his books and paperwork, and I shifted my books and paperwork upstairs from the living room. All I had to do was clear off the desk and begin working.

Less than five minutes in, you'd think I'd been handed a shovel and told to muck out the Augean stables. The grumbling began as soon as I dove into the tower of textbooks, worksheets, and lesson plans. It continued as I tackled the stack that comprised old calendars, expired car-service flyers, and cards from my fiftieth birthday. I couldn't seem to get through it all, even though I now had a big, spacious place for everything and my dad had always assured me that there is "a place for everything, and everything in its place." But I whined at every turn.

And then the bag I had been tossing old papers into split and erupted its contents all over the floor in a volcanic plume. Then the books I'd placed on the shelves crashed over and spilled to the ground—not even in the alphabetical order I'd organized them in. Meanwhile, the essay I'd begun (about annoying people in the medical field) wasn't working out because my vocabulary would not come when summoned, and the station I had playing on Pandora was irritating (who told Barbra Streisand she could sing?). I banged my fists. I stomped my feet. I yelled out bad words. The cat fled the room. Why was life so unfair?

To calm myself, I visited my daughter's blog. Her last few posts were about cheese, snow days, and happiness. Oh so cheery. Wishing everyone a happy Friday and an inspired March. Oh, please. How could she write about such wonderfulness? What made her so perky? Why wasn't she writing about her stupid subway ride home or how hard it was to start her own business in a shaky economy?

Finally, *finally*, dear reader, a big cosmic hand cut through my haze of self-pity and smacked me on the forehead. What the hell was wrong with me, anyway? What was I complaining about? Of course my daughter is perky—she's an energetic and enterprising young woman who is doing what she wants to do. And I was in the process of clearing a space in my very own home so I would have a private place to write—a move suggested by my supportive husband so I wouldn't have to work in the middle of the living room. And oh, yeah, I got to spend all morning doing this because I wasn't stuck at a nine-to-five job, working my tail off for someone else; I had the luxury of time to follow my dreams. Is that what I was complaining about?

Well, yes, I suppose it was. And yes, it was pitiful, but I'm better now. I'm fortunate enough to have people in my life who remind me how lucky I am without ever saying a word. No one yells at me, no one scolds me—they're just there, being themselves. So, even though some hippies with a dog have already memorialized this on T-shirts and other 100-percent-cotton accessories, let me say this: life is good. And shame on me for forgetting that.

Virtual Fitness

I never, ever get up early and think to myself, *What a great morning to exercise!* I am not an exercise person. I have exercised before in my life, and I own the various multicolored accoutrements to prove it. Lime-green and midnight-blue exercise bands. An enormous, silvery rubber ball. Slate-gray dumbbells. Bright red ropes with handles and attachments for ease of mounting on doors or other sturdy objects, so that when you pull on them you don't fall down. I own books, large and small, on easy-to-do yoga, quick fat-burning walks, five-minute core building, and toning my, er, everything. But am I toned? Nope.

A while back, my husband found a new app for his iPod called MyFitnessPal. He thought it would be great for us.

"You'll love it," he said.

"I won't," I said.

But he prevailed. And because of his commitment to fitness and his desire to exercise more, when he next started hinting about the new Xbox Kinect, I bought it for him for his birthday. (I know. I'm the nicest wife ever.) We played around with the two games we had (also purchased by the nicest wife ever) and discovered that even the "mini-games" wore us out, so my husband bought a personal-trainer game to help us get into better shape. He was much better at it than I was—shocking—but I did a few of the activities myself, and, much to my surprise, I found myself liking them.

One morning I woke up early, and as I lay in the comfort of a Bob-O-Pedic mattress, covered by a toasty-warm electric blanket, a strange thought occurred to me: *Why don't I get up and exercise?* I looked around to see who'd said it, but I was the only one there. So I got up and put on my sweatshirt and yoga pants. (Yes, I do have yoga pants even though I don't do yoga. It's good to have them, just in case.) I went downstairs, turned on the Xbox, and faced the Kinect sensor—it identified me, probably because of the yoga pants—and then, with my personal trainer, I began a rousing session of Stack 'Em Up.

Let me clue you in to how the Kinect works, because it's pretty fascinating. There are no controllers for this game system. *I* am the controller. The flat little black box with one red eye and one green one scans me up and down and records my image somewhere in its complex Xbox brain so it can recognize me when I want to use it. When I perform the exercises, an image of me appears on the screen so I can see exactly how uncoordinated I am when mirroring the "instructor's" motions. I can also see my cat on the screen when she prowls over to see what the hell I'm doing. She doesn't understand that when I hold my arm out to my side, it's not because I want to pet her, it's because I'm holding up a virtual balance board to catch all the falling blocks stacking up and giving me points.

I often drop the blocks at the wrong moment, and they crash and burn into the wrong bin. That's when the instructor says to me, "You're not really doing it right." Fortunately for her, she's virtual, so I can't slap her. She also said to me once, "Hey! Where are you going?" when all I wanted to do was drink some water and make some chocolate holiday bark. But I came back. Eventually.

So: exercising on purpose. Imagine that. And my husband and I can do it together. I totally kick his ass in Virtual Smash, but he's better than I am at most everything else. Hopefully the Kinect won't go the way of the exercise bands, yoga DVDs, and dumbbells. For now, it's fun. And I hear there's a Harry Potter game for Kinect. Maybe playing that is like exercising, too.

Work, Work, Work

I need a job. I know this is a familiar cry these days, but the fact is that although I need a job, I don't really *want* a job. Don't get me wrong; it's not that I don't want to work. I love to work. I work all the time. It's just that the kind of work I do doesn't really afford me the benefits I know and love. Like insurance, or an income.

Here's what it does afford me, though: the freedom to do just about anything I want to. As long as you don't count shopping for a new car or buying clothes as "anything," that is. But seriously, I am a pretty lucky girl: I am able to eat, stay warm, and keep the lights on. The first and main reason I am able to do this is my husband. He struck out on his own a couple of years before I quit my job and slowly but surely built up a private therapy–public visitation practice that does quite nicely, thank you. Since I work with him doing the visitations, we call it our "mom-and-pop" business. Cute, aren't we?

Over the years I've also picked up a couple of English classes to teach at our community college, which I love (who gets to be an adjunct with no day job?), and I've held on to a couple of other gigs that come with a paycheck. "Paycheck" may be too strong a word, actually—but there *is* a stipend involved with being a diversity trainer and computer/writing instructor. I do a few volunteer activities for my public library as well, and I'm a member of the oldest organization in Watertown, Connecticut, besides the Masons. It's a women's literary society founded in 1886. I'd tell you more, but then I'd have to kill you.

If I got "real" employment, of course, I'd have to give up all the odd jobs and community comings and goings. And they're what allow me to give the best of myself, because it's work I've chosen to do. I'm pretty sure a full-time employer would require me to show up on a regular basis, like, daily. And they might make me do stuff I don't like doing. That is what real jobs entail. At this point in my senescence, I've grown very fond of making my own schedule and spending lots and lots of time in my home and with my husband. (No, really, it's possible to do this without wanting to strangle each other on most days.) I also attend a writing group that meets during the day—whenever we want, wherever we want. At a Borders coffee shop, the local bagel place, anywhere. How in the world could I give all this up? I don't think I could. Because I would miss moments like this one:

I recently became addicted to a beverage called a Skinny Vanilla Latte. Ever hear of it? It is crazy delicious. They sell it at Starbucks, and you can get one as long as you're preapproved for a loan. I discovered it one day when I had a coupon for a free drink—any size—so I ordered myself one. Yum. I was hooked. On one of my designated writing days, I decided to treat myself to another one—you know, for inspiration. Or motivation. Whatever.

I went into the local shop and walked up to the counter. Cranky Barista was there, but so was Hippie Barista, and it was she who took my order. I asked for a Skinny Vanilla Latte, and then I leaned in close and asked quietly, "Do you put crack in these?"

Hippie Barista's eyes widened for a second. "Do we put . . . what? Crack?" She said it a little loudly.

"Usually I'm a black-coffee-and-Splenda girl," I quickly explained before Cranky Barista could call the cops, "but I ordered an SVL the other day, and now I can't get enough!"

"Oh, that's funny," Hippie Barista chuckled. "I needed that." As she put in the order, she asked slyly, "Do you want extra crack in that?"

"Yes, please," I said.

She continued chuckling and repeating, "Oh, I needed that today. . . . "

I moved to the pickup zone and waited a few minutes for my fix. On my way back past the counter, SVL in hand, Hippie Barista called me over.

"Did you get your pastry?" she asked.

"Oh, I didn't order a pastry," I replied, wondering if, in my junkie state, I was now having pastry blackouts and recklessly ordering raspberry scones and morning buns.

"Do you want one?" she whispered conspiratorially.

Oh. I get it. I smiled. "No, thanks, I'm fine." Since I had already pocketed a couple of extra Splendas, I didn't feel like I needed any extra loot. But I did think, *Isn't that sweet that she wants to slip me a contraband cupcake?* I had made her day, and now she wanted to make mine. A lovely, symbiotic instance that I might have missed if I hadn't been doing work I love.

Maybe I'll become a barista.

Fifteen Minutes of Fame

"In the future, everyone will be world-famous
for fifteen minutes."
—Andy Warhol

When I was little, I used to stay up late at night and watch *The Tonight Show* with Johnny Carson. I used to imagine sitting on the couch across the desk from him, engaging in lively and somewhat risqué banter, while inconspicuously tugging my beautifully sequined dress over my knees and demurely crossing my elegant, sparkly-heeled feet.

Why was I being interviewed? My fantasy didn't include those nonessential details. All I know is that I held Johnny in thrall—he hung on my every word while I smiled and chatted and talked about . . . well, again, who knows? But I was delightful.

Many years, and several *Tonight Show* hosts later, I had not been on Johnny's, Jay's, or anyone else's late-night talk show. I'd laid low all my life—raising children, teaching some folks, and posting my essays on my website. I hadn't done anything, it appears, that anyone would ever want to interview me for or put me before a camera as a result of.

Until now.

Some of the folks I teach are members of the over-fifty crowd—the AARP set, retirees. I teach a journal-writing course, and mostly it's a fun way to dig into parts of life that often remain unexcavated. One day a former student from that class emailed me and said he had met some folks who wanted to put together a variety show with local writers, poets, and musicians, and he asked if I would be interested in reading some of my work.

"Sure," I said, "count me in."

I had to audition, which was nerve-racking—but it was also kind of fun, and a few days later I heard that I was in the lineup for the first ever "First Thursday" performance. And it would be videotaped.

As all of this reading and auditioning had been a bit of a whirlwind, I hadn't realized at the outset that this venture was the brainchild of a couple who had recently moved to the States from Britain and who were interested in starting up another TV business in Connecticut like they had back in the UK. I'd thought it was just going to be videotaped for posterity's sake, not for commercial purposes! But I was game.

The night of the show, I was nervous. I usually don't mind being nervous, because it keeps me on my toes, and that way I don't make any really huge mistakes—only lots of little ones. (Like, I might keep playing with my hair, but I won't forget to read a whole page.) I was scheduled to go on second, after the host's intro and the first vignette—a scene from a play. I had to walk through the kitchen and time my entrance so it occurred between the exit of the actress from the scene before and the possibility of the host's coming back out to introduce me. He didn't. So, unannounced, I stepped out from behind the curtain—and into the lights. And cameras.

I wish I could say that I took to it like a duck to water, but that would be a flat-out lie. During the rehearsal, the director told me to remember to look at the camera, and the sound person reminded me to speak directly into the microphone. I forgot all of that as I stepped up to the mic and introduced myself. After that, everything was a blur. . . .

Except that it was videotaped, so I'm on film. The producers initially told us that they'd have the footage online for us to see, but, after obsessively checking the website every few minutes on the day it was supposed to launch, I forgot about it.

Then one day, I got the email that it was live—that I was on the Internet and potentially the whole world could see me. This was my fifteen minutes of fame. (Actually, it was my nine minutes and thirty-eight seconds of fame, but I'm okay with that.) The first time I watched it, I closed my eyes, just peeking a little, as if I were watching a *Scream* marathon. Then I watched it again, eyes open, and I didn't hate it. I kind of liked it, in fact.

The whole world didn't see me, of course. Probably only the people whom I directed to watch the video saw me—and it's a good bet that not even all of them saw it. But that's okay. In the bucket list of life, it's one more thing that I get to say I've done. In fact, it might even be the thing I lead with.

Spring Cleaning

Spring is a time of year when I have to be very careful with whom I strike up a conversation, because many of my friends and acquaintances tend to have these long and detailed discussions about a topic that, quite honestly, strikes fear into my heart. You know what I'm talking about: spring cleaning.

Don't get me wrong—I am generally in favor of cleaning. It's just that I don't want to do it. Actually, it's not even that I don't want to do it. I just can't. I don't have the coordination, patience, or attention span to *plan* to clean.

I think it would be pertinent and ironic to mention at this point that one summer I supported my family in part by cleaning other people's homes. These poor people didn't know about my deficiencies, nor was there any reason to tell them. Fortunately for them, I was merely bucket-holder and mop-toter to a frighteningly tidiness-obsessed woman who knew how to sweep through a home and leave it literally tingling with cleanliness. I simply followed her through the houses, holding and toting.

These spring-cleaning conversations that I refer to reveal people who take a, well, *psychopathic* thrill in chasing down dust bunnies to their deaths. I was having coffee with my friend (and writers' group) Trudy one day, for example, and she mentioned that she needed to get home and wash her kitchen floor. I was floored. She did that? Like, got a bucket and sponges and some kind of cleaning fluid and planned to wash the floor . . . like, all at once? Not with a damp paper towel when she spilled some spaghetti sauce? I was both impressed and baffled. I believe I had the same confused look on my face as I did when my friend Sue once said to me, "Sorry I was late; I had to iron my blouse," and I had to ask, "What's an iron?"

But back to this cleaning thing. Spring cleaning is an age-old tradition—I'm told—and it's a practice that is especially prevalent in climates with a cold winter. (It's true, I swear—I looked it up on Wikipedia.) In another ironic turn, I found that this activity apparently finds its roots in the Persian new year celebration of Norooz—a celebration I've attended. We did not clean at this celebration. We ate and drank. It was fun. The only things I held and toted were beverages and plates of Persian delicacies.

Now, before you all shrink back in horror and make a mental note to never, ever come visit me, rest assured: my house is not about to be condemned by the health department. I'm not a reality show. The problem is that I've *tried* to clean, but I just can't do it. Here's an example: In the spring of 2012 I realized that my husband had not replaced the mini-blinds in my bedroom with new, darker ones, as I thought he had. The beige ones we put up when we moved in were still hanging in place; it's just that they needed a good cleaning. The new color wasn't a new color at all—it was dust. And, embarrassingly, it was several years' worth of dust. I'd always thought that raising them up and down shook the dust off—a sort of self-cleaning function—but this was not the case.

In my defense, I have hired cleaning ladies on various occasions, and they apparently don't do blinds, either. I'd rather not talk about the cleaning ladies, however: they were my husband's idea, I didn't want them in my house, and it was a painful and horrifying experience for me. When they came, I had to attempt, in my challenged way, to get the house in order and then flee to another state while they were in my home. And yet they didn't even clean the mini-blinds. I suppose they thought the blinds were self-cleaning, too.

It was clear that this chore was up to me.

The first task was getting them down from the windows. There were three different kinds of hardware holding them in place, so it was difficult three different times. I had prepared my cleaning supplies—a full bottle of cleanser, a brush, a sponge—and I took them all outside to the front yard where the hose is connected. I will spare you the ugly details, but suffice it to say that an activity that would have taken most people about twenty minutes to complete took me over an hour. First I couldn't decide whether to clean the blinds fully extended or fully collapsed (neither was very manageable); then I had to figure out how to dry them. Finally, I hung the once-beige mini blinds over the side of my porch to dry and took in my handiwork. And they looked worse than they had when I had taken them down. Seriously. They looked like I'd taken them outside and thrown dirt on them.

So I'm done with spring cleaning. I'm not talking about it, I'm not worrying about it, I'm not doing it. It's a nice concept for those among us who have some coordination and endurance, but for those of us who don't—and I'm mostly just talking about me, here—it's enough to simply pull down the shades when the morning sun streams in and highlights the dust on my bookshelves. Besides, I've discovered a plastic container that dispenses handy wipes for cleaning almost anything—wood, bathrooms, windows, babies, you name it. They're better than ketchup in a squeeze bottle, and they keep the health department at bay.

And who wants to talk about cleaning anyway?

I Don't Have Much, But I Love What I've Got

A while back, I received—or bought—an orchid. (It may have been a gift, but I don't remember. One of the things I don't have much of is memory.) It bloomed on the table in the kitchen for months, until, one by one, the delicate petals fell off, leaving only broad, waxy leaves and a creepy-looking stem held to a stake by a small plastic hair clasp. I didn't want to toss it out in the garbage—that seemed harsh. It had been so pretty, and I marveled at the fact that I hadn't killed it before its apparently natural demise. I Googled "orchids" to see if I could nurture it back to beauty once more.

I wasn't too hopeful.

As it turned out, there were some easy "bring back to life" instructions on a website I found. So, as per the site's advice, I cut back the creepy-looking stem, added some fertilizer, and waited. A couple of months later, what looked like an exposed root started to poke upward. It slowly turned from brown to green, and as it grew I used the hair clasp to secure it to the stake. I continued to water it, and eventually a tiny green shoot appeared with a small greenish bulb at the end. Then more appeared—I was getting excited—and then it bloomed. I came down one morning and saw delicate pink blossoms hanging from the tiny stems.

Success! And there were more blooms after that—and, later, a stronger-looking stem as well. I pointed it out, more than once, to everyone who walked through the kitchen: "Look! It came back! It came back!" My family was not overly thrilled. But I felt like I'd just painted the Sistine Chapel.

My point is that there is a lot that I can't do. And once one gets to a certain age, it's not likely that she is going to acquire many more skills and abilities than those she already possesses. Old dog, new tricks—that sort of thing. Some people can grow acres and acres of flora and fauna; I can't. But I *can* get one orchid to come back. And that makes me happy. I like what I am able to do, and I'm grateful for what I am able to do. And I'm grateful for what others can do that I can't, like preparing my taxes and putting a roof on my house. It's nice to be at a stage of life in which I don't feel like I have to do everything. I can just do the stuff that I can do—as well as I can do it—and let other people do the stuff *they* can do.

Why have all the fun to myself?

Acknowledgments

Thank you to so many.

My whole family: Warren, Pattie, Richard, Susan, Stephan and John. Thank you for your strength, honesty, creativity, support, and love. All the time. Whether I needed it or not.

To my husband and children: Angelo, Annie, Christopher, Justine, Tony and Luca. You all are a part of this inaugural effort, and your stories are in these very pages. No effort is worthwhile without you.

Thank you to my writers' group, Trudy. Thank you for pushing me to bring my dream into reality. You are an incomparable friend and confidant, and I am forever grateful.

About the Author

Cindy Eastman is a writer and an educator.

Born in Bridgeport, Connecticut in 1958, Cindy was raised in Louisville, Kentucky. She attended undergraduate schools in Austin, Texas and graduate school in Springfield, Massachusetts and holds a master's degree in Education. After writing a weekly column for the Waterbury Observer, she began publishing essays on her website, Writing Out Loud.

Her career in education has taken a wide and diverse route from teaching computer skills to elementary schoolchildren to facilitating professional learning communities for teachers and teaching English as an adjunct to college freshmen at a community college.

Eastman's work is informed by her ability to be an observer as well as a participant in her life. Starting at an early age, she kept journals to record her encounters – and make up stories – about the people, places and events that she experienced. The stories began to take a backseat to her observations, which became more and more fine-tuned as valid commentary on human behavior. With her dry sense of humor, she is able to address a variety of topical subjects and deliver an insightful analysis that's both provocative and amusing.

Currently, she coordinates a supervised visitation service with her husband in his counseling practice and does diversity and anti-bullying trainings for the Anti-Defamation League. She also teaches a writing course for the Osher Lifelong Learning Institute at the Waterbury campus of UConn.

She says, "I turned fifty a couple of years ago, and it suddenly became important to me to do work that is significant to who I am and what's important to me. I am a writer--still 'emerging' in my fifties--but a writer all the same. The way I look at things is both broad and intense. I can see the big picture and all the little specks on the floor. Although it doesn't make me a better housekeeper, this ability allows me to synthesize those pictures into universal observations with which others may identify."

Eastman makes her home in Connecticut with her husband, Angelo, and their cat. She is working on a second collection of essays when she is not babysitting her grandson.

SELECTED TITLES FROM SHE WRITES PRESS

*She Writes Press is an independent publishing company
founded to serve women writers everywhere.
Visit us at www.shewritespress.com.*

*A Tight Grip: A Novel about Golf, Love Affairs, and Women of a
Certain Age* by Kay Rae Chomic $16.95, 978-1-938314-76-6
As forty-six-year-old golfer Jane "Par" Parker prepares for her next
tournament, she experiences a chain of events that force her to reevaluate her life.

Duck Pond Epiphany by Tracey Barnes Priestley
$16.95, 978-1-938314-24-7
When a mother of four delivers her last child to college, she has to
decide what to do next—and her life takes a surprising turn.

Warming Up by Mary Hutchings Reed
$16.95, 978-1-938314-05-6
Unemployed and depressed former musical actress Cecilia Morrison
decides to start therapy, hoping it will get her out of her slump—but
ultimately it's a teen who cons her out of sixty bucks, not her analyst,
who changes her life.

Class Letters: Instilling Intangible Lessons through Letters
by Claire Chilton Lopez $16.95, 978-1-938314-28-5
A high school English teacher discovers surprising truths about her
students when she exchanges letters with them over the course of a
school year.

Loveyoubye: Hanging On, Letting Go, and Then There's the Dog
by Rossandra White $16.95, 978-1-938314-50-6
A soul-searching memoir detailing the painful, but ultimately liberating, disintegration of a twenty-five-year marriage.

Seeing Red: A Woman's Quest for Truth, Power, and the Sacred
by Lone Morch $16.95, 978-1-938314-12-4
One woman's journey over inner and outer mountains—a quest that
takes her to the holy Mt. Kailas in Tibet, through a seven-year marriage, and into the arms of the fierce goddess Kali, where she discovers
her powerful, feminine self.

3|19

CPSIA information can be obtained
at www.ICGtesting.com
Printed in the USA
BVOW08s2123120617
486723BV00001B/5/P